African Art

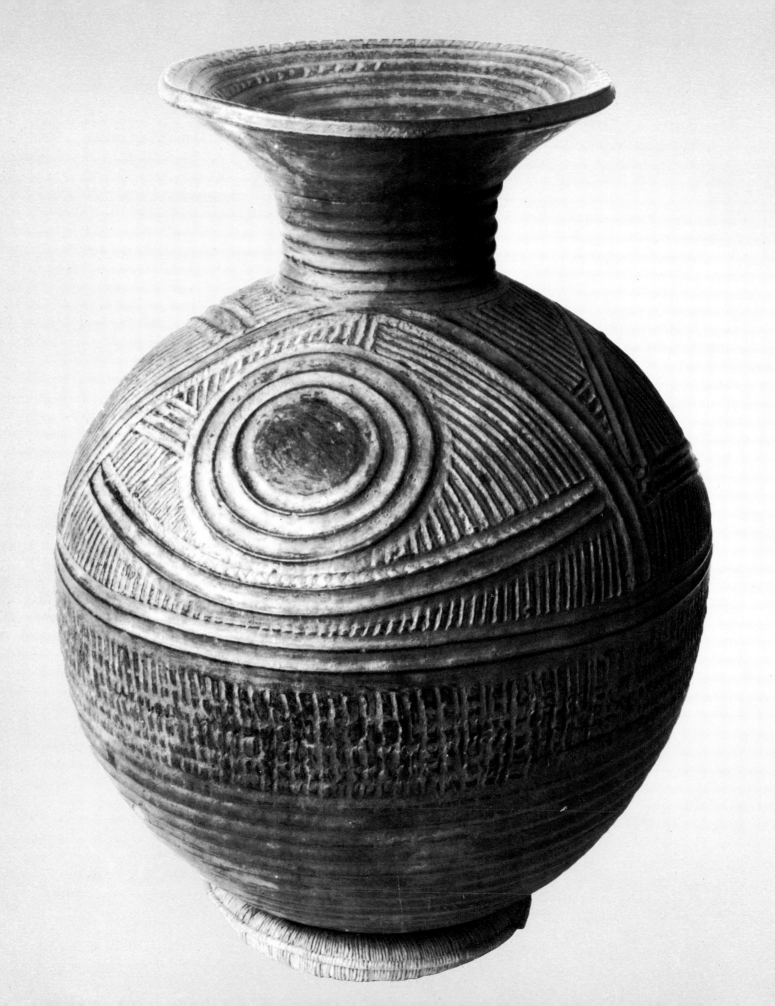

Dennis Duerden

African Art

The Colour Library of Art

Hamlyn

London · New York · Sydney · Toronto

Acknowledgments

The objects and paintings in this volume are reproduced by kind permission of the following collections, galleries and museums to which they belong: Jimo Akolo (Plate 47); American Museum of Natural History, New York (Plate 3); Professor David Arnott Collection, London (Figure 7); Yemi Bisiri (Plate 49); British Museum, London (Plates 13, 17, 21, 22, 30, 31, 32, 39, Figures 3, 4, 5); Michael Cardew Collection, Bodmin (Figure 1); Professor Gellner Collection, London (Plate 44); Peggy Guggenheim Collection, Venice (Plate 9); Horniman Museum, London (Plate 40, Figure 2); Ife Museum, Nigeria (Plate 28); Jos Museum, Nigeria (Plates 29a, 29b); Raymond Lecoq, Présence Africaine, Paris (Figure 8); Dr. G. Liersch Collection, Munich (Plate 45); Linden-Museum, Stuttgart (Plates 4, 36, Figure 6); Josef Muller Collection, Solothurn (Plate 23); Musée de l'Homme, Paris (Plates 2, 6); Museum of Primitive Art, New York (Plate 12); Museum Rietberg, Zurich (Plates 1, 18); Museum Rietberg, Zurich, Edouard van der Heydt Collection (Plates 7, 24, 26); Museum für Völkerkunde, Berlin-Dahlem (Plates 5, 14); Asiru Olatunde (Plate 50); Morris J. Pinto Collection, Paris (Plate 8); M. Charles Ratton Collection, Paris (Plate 10); Rhodes National Gallery, Salisbury, Rhodesia (Figure 9); Ibrahim Salahi (Plate 46); Twins Seven-Seven (Plate 48); H. Christophe Tzara Collection, Paris (Plate 15); M. Pierre Vérité Collection, Paris (Plate 11); Zurich University Ethnological Collection (Plates 16, 25).

The following photographs were supplied by: Paul Almasy, Paris (Plates 19, 20, 28); Professor Julian Beinart, Cape Town (Plates 41, 42, 43); Corry Bevington, London (Plate 37); Heinz Binder, Stuttgart (Plates 4, 36); Donald Bowen, London (Figure 9); Ed. Duchêne (Rapho Paris) (Plate 27); Dennis Duerden, London (Plate 45); Bernard Fagg, Oxford (Plates 29a, 29b); Ferruzzi, Venice (Plate 9); Michael Holford, London (Plates 13, 17, 21, 22, 30, 32, 39, 40, 46, 47, 48, 49, 50, Figures 2, 3, 4, 5); Holle and Co. Verlag, Baden-Baden (Plates 1, 7); Michael Lancaster, London (Plates 33, 34, 35); Raymond Laniepce, Paris (Plates 8, 10); J. A. Lavaud, Paris (Plates 2, 11, 15); Oskar Luz, Tübingen (Plate 51); E. Muller-Rieder, Zurich (Plates 23, 24, 25, 26); Sargent/Gamma Studios, Guildford (Figure 1); F. Seebach, London (Plate 38); Charles Uht, New York (Plate 12); Wettstein und Kauf, Zurich (Plate 18). Frontispiece. Gwazunu Pot. Terracotta. Height 15 in. (38 cm.). Collection of Michael Cardew, Bodmin.

The Hamlyn Publishing Group also wishes to thank the following authors and publishers for permission to quote extracts from their books:
Chinua Achebe *Arrow of God* (William Heinemann Ltd);
J. W. Abruquah *The Catechist* (George Allen & Unwin Ltd);
Wole Soyinka *The Swamp Dwellers* (Oxford University Press);
Amos Tutuola *Simbi and the Satyr* (Faber & Faber Ltd).

First Published 1968
Paperback Edition 1970
Published by The Hamlyn Publishing Group Limited
Hamlyn House, Feltham, Middlesex, England
© Paul Hamlyn Ltd 1968

ISBN 0 600 03743 6

Printed in Italy by Officine Grafiche Arnoldo Mondadori, Verona

Contents

Introduction

AFRICAN ART AND THE SAHARA

In the continent of Africa indigenous art is found almost exclusively south of the Sahara desert; to the north are the Islamic countries whose art resembles that of the Middle East and the Arab world. There are some connections between African art south of the Sahara and that found in early Egyptian sites, but in general the art discussed here was driven out of North Africa a thousand years ago. Some areas in the southern, eastern and western regions of the Sahara were converted to Islam. They are referred to geographically as the Savannah areas of Africa and are characterised by plains of long grass and stunted trees. The Sudanic Empires which were found there were converted to Islam between the seventh and the fourteenth centuries. They raided for slaves into the forests to the south, but were never able to penetrate very far because their armies were mounted and horses were unable to travel in the thick forest, nor could they survive there because of the tsetse fly. However, although the rulers of the Savannah area south of the Sahara were converted to Islam, many groups of people in these areas were either imperfectly converted or remained unconquered because they lived in rocky hills or plateaux which provided a natural defence against the invading horsemen. So the art of the old African religions flourished even in the Savannah areas conquered by Islam. The old art and the old religions are associated with the more typical social organisation in Africa south of the Sahara, which seems to be the product of the conditions of life in the thick forest. It is as if the large centralised kingdom and empires derived from the Savannah areas, and a diffused system of family groups was necessary in the forests. The fact that social organisations based on family groups are also found spread over the Savannah areas is perhaps evidence that a long time ago the area of forest vegetation was very much greater than it is now.

SOCIAL ORGANISATION IN THE RAIN FORESTS

Most of the examples of African societies described in this introductory essay are taken from Nigeria. The best studies of art in African societies have been made there, some of the most illuminating descriptions having come from Nigerian authors. It seems best therefore to consider the place of art in society in the context of one area, and then to consider a number of other examples in the rest of Africa. The other examples will be given in the notes to the plates.

The study of an Ibo community in the rain forest of Eastern Nigeria will give us a prototype of social organisation in the African forests. Such an Ibo community is described by Margaret Green in her book *Ibo Village Life*. She lived in an Ibo village in Eastern Nigeria in 1936 and 1937 and so was able to observe what life was like there before it was radically changed by the Christian Missions. She describes a village of almost 150 people which belonged to a group of eleven villages. The eleven villages traced their descent from a common ancestor, and the families in each single village in the group traced their descent to the sons of the group ancestor. The village itself was divided into two halves and each half was said to be descended from the son of one of two wives of the village ancestor. In each half there were two or three lineage groups or 'houses'. Each lineage group worshipped its own ancestral spirit and a man was chosen to carry its *ofo* or sacred staff. A half village or a whole village rarely united together for any purpose except to fight a war against another village. Similarly the whole group of villages never united except for war against another group of villages. Every year the men of each village would join together to cut a path to the big central market of the village group, but each group of men would make sure they left the market place before the men from the next village arrived in case they should start fighting. Whenever the women from a village went to another market they would sit near the path by which they came in order to be able to get away quickly in case fighting broke out. The married women of the villages, however, all came from other villages because exogamy was the rule. The practical reason for this marriage outside the village was to ensure that families would still have a means of communicating with one another and trading in case of war. It was a case of trade following the women.

There was great danger of children and even adults being lost in the thick forest which intruded everywhere, and for this reason the people of the village would continually call to one another, even in the middle of conversation, answering the calls of others who wanted to establish where they were. If a stranger came into the village everyone would suddenly disappear. However, communications were kept over large distances by the *dibia* or diviners who were consulted on every matter of birth, life and death. The *dibia* from all the villages for as much as a hundred miles apart would have regular meetings and exchange knowledge of their mysteries. Their function was to tell people to which spirits they should make sacrifices, what names to give their children, what taboos they should observe, and so forth. Even so, in this matter of consulting the *dibia* everyone exercised great freedom of choice, and if a *dibia* did not please the individual's personal tastes, then that person might go to another who seemed to him more knowledgeable or more powerful. As each family group had an ancestral spirit, so each village, each village group, each river, each forest grove, might have its own guardian spirits. One of the tasks of the *dibia* was to advise on the choices to be made from this pantheon of deities. Each spirit in the pantheon had its priest who was responsible for ensuring that the correct sacrifices were offered, that its devotees observed its correct taboos, and other matters. The priests brought out carved images of their spirits once a year at the season assigned to them when their devotees would celebrate with sacrifices, chanting and dancing. During the rest of the year the images would not be seen. This then is one example of a society living in the forest and organised in lineage groups, found all over those parts of Africa which produced the art of the masks and the carved figures which we know under the general title of African art. It was a society of individualists who rarely came together except for festivals or for fighting. There was great rivalry and jealousy between the two halves of the village, as Margaret Green discovered. The villagers in the Ibo community in which she lived built a house for her, but neither side considered itself bound by agreements unless the elders of both halves had been present at discussions; even within a kindred there would be complaints that only the senior man was called for discussion and that he should not have been singled out. Not all African societies were as divided as this one. But even if this is regarded as an extreme case, all other systems of traditional government in Africa seem to be superimposed on a cellular social organisation of this kind; and all societies have pantheons of deities in which the gods or spirits represent each social cell. Moreover, the masks and figures which represent these gods and spirits are seldom brought out more than once a year; then they are hidden away until they are needed again. This brings us to a very important point about traditional African art and the difficulties it presents to the European in his approach to it.

EUROPEANS AND AFRICAN ART

When we look at African sculpture in a museum, in a private house or in a photograph, we are separating a work of art from its environment, thereby preventing ourselves from understanding its significance to its creator. Most African works of art are created for use in ceremonies performed to induce particular states of mind in the people. For their creators their meaning lies in the part they play in these ceremonies, together with the kindred arts of music, dancing and poetry. They are brought out of hiding and used in danced masquerades or kept in shrines and only seen by the people during special ceremonies conducted by priests. Some people keep images for use in family ceremonies, but these are never seen by the rest of the community. African works of art are seldom available to the community as a whole, in contrast to the European practice of decorating their churches before public museums were organised. In the past some romantic writers on primitive art have argued that in pre-industrial societies art is available to and understood by the whole of the community. They claim that after the industrial revolution in our society the people became alienated from sources of works of art and ceased to understand the language of art. The African sculptor is supposed to use a symbolism understood by everyone in his village. In fact the African sculptor creates works which are used in very difficult and complicated mysteries. His art is just as inaccessible to the majority of people as the most avant-garde painting or sculpture in our own society. This romantic theory of an art understood by the whole community is usually offered to explain why the African artist who has been educated in an industrial society no longer does work similar to that produced in pre-industrial society. It seems more probable that the accomplished artist in a pre-industrial society, whether he is a sculptor, a poet, a musician or a dancer, is the possessor of rare talents who goes through a long and difficult period of training; and it is obvious that a similar training is not available to the African painter who goes to a modern art school. The pre-industrial artist is a man who not only spends years and years in strenuous apprenticeship learning how to use his tools and his materials; he has an intimate knowledge of the ceremonies for which he designs his work, and those other arts and lore connected with them. As a rule the climax of a ceremony comes with the principal performer in a state of trance or performing some spectacular feat, such as an act of prophesy. The offering of a sacrifice coincides with the climax. The sacrifice is extremely important: for example, a dog is sacrificed to Ogun, the Yoruba cult-god of War and Iron every year. Of this sacrifice Ulli Beier writes (see book list on page 32):

'The sacrifice of a dog is not easy to witness for one who has been brought up with the European attitude towards dogs. It is most revealing, however, to experience the tremendous release of tension that accompanies the sacrifice. The tension and concentration of the worshippers mount incessantly during the lengthy preparations. Then as soon as the blood flows, everyone breaks into a relaxed dance.'

Ulli Beier describes another ceremony in which there is a gradual build-up of tremendous tension. This time the tension is achieved by a young girl walking to the river with a kola nut in her mouth. She walks to the river for about a mile surrounded by people dancing, chanting and drumming in an ever increasing tempo. When she reaches the river she takes the kola nut out of her mouth and prophesies what the town must do during the coming year. This is the ceremony of the river goddess, Oshun.

These sacrifices are used to rid the participants of socially dangerous emotions. Even the Yoruba, who have long since been converted to Christianity, feel the need for sacrifices, and are surprised that Europeans do not.

It is easy therefore to understand the essential difference between African and European attitudes to these same works of art. The African in a traditional society who actually made them and used them regards them as adjuncts to a ceremony in which a release of tension takes place and dangerous social passions are released and relaxed. To the European they are objects of contemplation and they are rarely, if ever, considered together with the drumming, dancing, chanting and sacrificing which originally formed their context and which were so very important at the time.

IMPERMANENCE OF AFRICAN ART

In Africa works of art are not destined for permanence, although many are very carefully preserved. They are often made of very soft wood and it is not considered a great loss if they are eventually eaten by termites. Carvings may be painted with the residue from the bottom of dye pits to preserve them, then wrapped in banana leaves and hung in the smoke from the fire. In this way they may last for about fifty years, but are probably considered more efficacious if they are then replaced. When new ones are made the sculptor performs various elaborate ceremonies to help him make a new vehicle for the gods to inhabit during the ceremonies. In fact a wide distinction is made between works of art which are relics of the past, such as the bronze head and figures which are occasionally discovered and those related to the immediate present. The historical relics are merely survivals from people in the remote past; the carvings in use today are an active means of bringing one's immediate ancestors into one's life. There is no precise boundary between life and death: the immediate forefathers are believed to be present all the time to advise and assist the living, but those who lived two or three hundred years earlier are felt to be strange and remote.

This emphasis on the present also conditions the African attitude to history. The history of the village in the tribe is constantly being revised to fit the present situation. Anything which would revive the memory of old quarrels is discarded. History is the record of those agreements which closely unite people in the present. It is regarded as sacrilege to probe into matters which may only inflame old feuds. History is merely a means of keeping the peace and the people united. It can never be objective.

It would be wrong to conclude, however, that because African carvings are renewed at least every fifty years, and because many thousands have been made during the past hundred years (recently William Fagg estimated that the Yoruba alone still have two million in their keeping), that African art today is necessarily quite different from what it was two thousand years ago. In fact there are great stylistic resemblances between, for example, the Nok terracottas which have been dug up on the plateau of Northern Nigeria and are estimated to be two thousand years old, and the soapstone figures at Esie, south of the River Niger, which are reputed to have been made in the eighteenth century. Moreover, the stylistic gulf between the Nok heads and modern Yoruba wood-carving is not very great.

COURT ART IN AFRICA

It would be mere generalisation to suggest that traditional African art is primarily concerned with maintaining the psychological balance of individuals in the community. It is not solely devoted to providing means whereby the spirits and the gods are brought into the midst of the living, although a vast amount does fulfil this function. Fifty years ago the number of masks and cult figures must have amounted to millions. Thousands of these are now preserved in museums and private collections in Africa and elsewhere, and many areas have been almost completely denuded of original work by collectors. There were fewer examples of other art forms to be found, but Africa was rich in the purely decorative arts and a certain amount of court monumental art was discovered.

When the first great finds were made, for example those of the 1897 expedition to the city of Benin, and the Ife heads re-discovered in 1910 by Leo Forbenius, they were judged by European experts to be works of art, probably because they were more representational. The abstract work, however, was considered to be of great ethnological interest, but of no artistic value. So powerful, indeed was the appeal of the Ife heads that it was even questioned by some that they could be the work of Africans. One of the more remarkable theories advanced to account for their origin was that they might have been made by some visiting Renaissance artist, because of their almost classical elegance.

The abstract work did not receive its full measure of appreciation until it was discovered by Picasso and Braque in Paris, and Kirchner and the Expressionists in Germany. Much later its influence became apparent in the work of Brancusi and Henry Moore, but it is only since about 1945 that its artistic merit has received its due.

The people who have produced the most representational art in Africa are the Kwa speakers, a group which includes the Beni and the Yoruba of Nigeria, the Fon of Dahomey, the Ewe of Togoland, and the Fanti and the Ashanti of Ghana. Kwa speakers apparently believe that a separate spirit resides in a man's head, and place great emphasis on the head as the seat of intelligence. In various ceremonies they make sacrifices to the head and these become increasingly important as the power of the man increases. The ceremonies and the sacrifices which the great kings dedicate to their heads are very large and very important. When sacrifices are made to the Oba of Benin's head the priests begin with a cock and place larger and larger animals on the pile until they finish with an elephant. The Oba sits in a kind of trance for about two hours while the ceremony is performed. Then he prophesies. Perhaps it is not too fanciful to suggest that all the skill and craftsmanship which went into the Ife heads was lavished on them to make them lasting monuments to the heads of great kings. They are about a thousand years old, but their likeness to the Yoruba in present day Nigeria is most striking.

The great kingdoms of Africa have, therefore, produced a type of art at their centres which is very different from that generally found in the villages and towns. The kings and their courts have tried to impress their power on the people they rule by having their likenesses and their histories made in more permanent materials and have had them erected where they can be seen. Their art is similar in purpose, though not in size, to the larger likenesses of the Pharaohs to be found in Egypt. The walls of the palace of the Oba of Benin were covered in the bronze plaques like that shown in plate 31. In areas where representational art was not so highly developed, the kings have contented themselves with erecting great palaces, the walls and entrances of which are decorated in a style which might almost be called baroque.

Large kingdoms, however, did not predominate in Africa, although modern historians have tended to emphasise the existence of such kingdoms and have exaggerated their

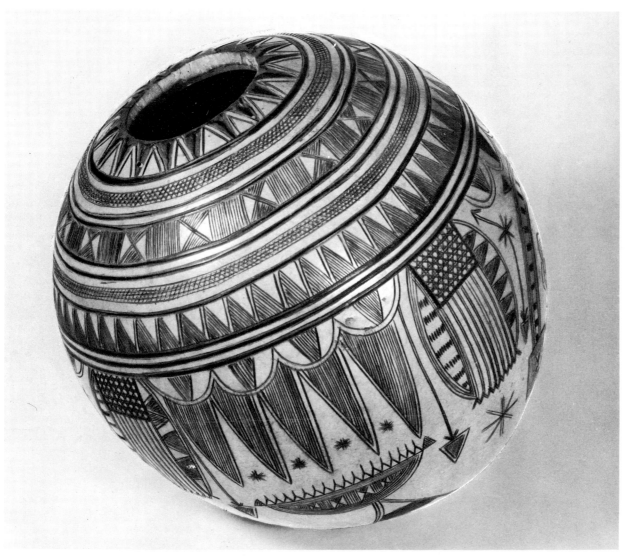

2. Scorched calabash. West Africa. Height 12 in. (30.5 cm.). Horniman Museum, London.

significance to counteract the still common belief that Africa had no civilisation. This belief has arisen partly because the African people themselves have not valued the relics of their civilisation; but the existence of great numbers of African works of art in museums and the richness of African languages and music disproves it. The languages of Africa with their wonderfully subtle poetry and the music of Africa with its complicated rhythms and counterpoints, which Western musicologists wonder at but still do not fully understand, would lead us to suppose that it is wrong to think that written histories, large buildings, monuments and relics of the past are the only evidences of civilisation. Perhaps there is another kind of civilisation which emphasises performance itself and does not require those who participate to leave evidence that they have participated. Its aesthetic canons would be rather like those we have come to expect from jazz musicians. It would look at the past from the present and not seek to understand what living in the past was like. It would not try to control the future, because the future would exist in the present. Some of this kind of thinking is summed up by an African philosopher who became a Fellow of All Souls College, Oxford, Professor William Abraham of the University of Ghana, in his book *The Mind of Africa*. Anyone who tries to struggle with its extremely difficult language may get some idea of what African 'civilisation' is about. However, it is irrelevant in this context to speculate on whether or not there was a civilisation in Africa, but it is relevant to point out that it would be a mistake to search diligently for traces of large buildings in Africa in an attempt to identify what a European would define as civilisation. It is possible that large buildings and monuments may have been erected by kings and emperors who sought to arrest time and to impose themselves in space, because their concepts of time and space were fundamentally different from those of the mass of their subjects. For the majority of people in traditional Africa the measure of time and space was that of the clan or the tribe; the more conspicuous and monumental forms of art were required by rulers who wished to emphasise their own permanence and universality above that of the tribe. The rulers of modern African states have been obliged to contend with a society in which clan loyalties are paramount. They have tried to do so by proclaiming their power in a highly exaggerated way like the kings of Ashanti, Ife and Benin in the past. It may be that an exactly similar problem faced Rameses II whose huge statue supports the temple at the Aswan dam. The past abounds in examples of African chiefs and generals who were obliged to call attention to their power in horrifying ways in order to assert themselves in the face of people's allegiance to the clan. Leo Frobenius tells the story of a Nupe general in Nigeria who sacrificed his two children and had their skins stretched on drums to show his power, a power which worked through him, but which was always available in the universe to be harnessed by those equipped to summon it by similar acts of defiance. The Kabaka of Uganda would quite arbitrarily send his wives to be executed in order to show that his power was working through him. Chaka of the Zulus caused his regiments to beat the waves with their assegais, because the waves would not obey his commands. The trance-like grimace of a chief in the grip of such power is shown in many African sculptures. But the chief's own people assisted him to power. A woman sacrificed by the Ashanti, among a large number of victims, escaped death and came back to tell the chief that the cult-gods would not accept her because she was not well enough dressed. Then she gladly accepted clothes and ornaments and was despatched more efficiently the second time. The Kabaka's wife went willingly to her execution and refused to have her hands tied. The more effectively power worked through the chief, the more his supporters would prosper. He symbolised their strength and security, the measure of which was reflected in the extremes to which he might go. The very arbitrariness of these acts increased the people's sense of security while at the same time inducing feelings of terror. The British who entered the Kingdom of Benin in 1897 and saw the streets running with blood and the decapitated bodies on the sacrificial trees were horrified, but the Oba of Benin's subjects merely felt secure that they were protected by such a powerful cult hero, who had carried so many people with him when he went to join their ancestors.

The idea of a force or power which may be summoned by chiefs or by cult priests is an important one in African metaphysics. It has been described as a kind of electricity inherent in all material objects and in all human beings. It can be unleashed with terrible fury or it can be harnessed for good, but there is also a strong element of luck to be taken into account. Yoruba who try to exercise it, for example, are always at the mercy of Eshu the trickster God. Some people seem fated from birth to misuse it, others to use it successfully. William Fagg has said that it is expressed in African sculpture by the exponential curve (as seen, for example, in the progressive curves of a snail shell). Many works of sculpture are constructed on the principal of the exponential curve and they symbolise the abstract force or power which resides in all things.

However, the King who tries to channel this force in order to impose his power on an Empire of one or two million people has always had to contend with the multiple divisions of African society. This is not to say that the clans and small communities in African societies are detached from the larger states: the society has remained permanently divided 'since the start of time itself'. This phrase is used in *The Swamp Dwellers*, a play by the modern Nigerian playwright, Wole Soyinka. A stranger comes to the village and wants to farm a piece of land which has always belonged to a cult-god who takes the form of a serpent.

Beggar	Is there land here which a man can till? Is there any land to spare for a man who is willing to give his soul to the soil?
Makuri	No, friend. All the land that can take the weight of a hoe is owned by someone in the village. Even the few sheep and goats haven't any land on which to graze. They have to be fed on cassava and other roots.
Beggar	But if a man is willing to take a piece of the ground and redeem it from the swamps – will they let him? If a man is willing to drain the filth away and make the land yield coco-yams and lettuce – will they let him?
Makuri	Mind what you are saying. Mind what profanities you utter in this house.
Beggar	I merely ask to be given a little of what land is useless to the people.
Makuri	You wish to rob the Serpent of the Swamps? You wish to take the food out of his Mouth?
Beggar	The Serpent! The Serpent of the Swamps?
Makuri	The land that we till and live on has been ours from the beginning of time. The bounds that are marked by ageless iroko trees that have lived since the birth of the

Serpent, since the birth of the world, since the start of time itself. What is ours is ours! But what belongs to the Serpent may never be taken from him.

It is because the king has had to try to impose his power on the elemental force in the thousands of divisions in African society that he has proclaimed his power with buildings, monuments and with alarming sacrifices. But the force in the coils of the serpent has always proved stronger than the sword in the hands of the king. The legend of the founding of the Hausa states in Northern Nigeria tells of a man who beheaded a serpent living in a well and became king. The Hausa states have remained seven nevertheless and the Fulani who conquered them in the early nineteenth century have perpetuated the division.

THE AFRICAN SCULPTOR

African society thus resembles a honeycomb of lineage groups and hidden in each cell of the honeycomb are the sources of their power, the cult objects, the statues and the masks. The statues and the masks are renewed every fifty years, but the lineage group remains. It has persisted for thousands of years and the forms of the statues have been handed on from generation to generation. Sometimes the cells unite and swear temporary allegiance to a king. The king brings his statues out from their hiding place, casts them in bronze and erects them where everyone can see them. Somehow the fixity of their gaze and the twisted rigidity of their bronze limbs has not arrested time for us so powerfully as the ancestral masks and the cult-gods of the single cells, the separate lineage groups.

The immortality of the lineage group is expressed in the sculpture of the cults. It is expressed in a public ceremony in which every man feels united to his ancestors and his own life or death is unimportant to him. At that moment when the past, the present and the future are all one, the form of the statue is important for increasing the sense of the unity of all in the lineage bond. Then the sacrifice is made, the timeless moment is created, the tension is broken, the ceremony has taken place and the mask or the statue can be put away until it is required again, perhaps not for another year. Its form is not contemplated and is only vaguely remembered.

It would not be true to say, however, that each lineage group has its own artist. It is commonly supposed that every African village has its sculptor, but in fact their number is probably comparatively small. People have travelled as much as a hundred miles to buy masks or sculpture for their cults, and the work of a particular sculptor with a particular workshop has become prized above others. In fact William Fagg has described how, among the Yoruba, the fame of certain sculptors has spread over a wide area. The work of Areogun or Bamgboye, for example, is readily identifiable from the style of the pieces now to be seen in museums. In other areas a particular tribe may be famed for its sculpture and neighbouring tribes may travel far to buy what they need from that particular tribe. Men from other families may come and serve as apprentices under the master sculptor and spend years carrying out menial tasks, cutting the trees in the forest, preparing the food, farming and building for the master, before they are allowed to work on any pieces of their own.

While the master carves a particular piece he may invoke by special ceremonies of his own those powers which he wants to work through the sculpture. When he comes to finish the work he must achieve just that state of trance-like concentration which the work itself is supposed to transmit to its beholders. He achieves the state of mind in which he can finish the work by using specially consecrated tools and by sacrifices to the cult-gods. So he is respected as a kind of priest, as a man with knowledge of important mysteries, and through whom the forces which are ultimately designed to inhabit the sculpture will work on it. The artist himself is a channel of communication with the supernatural: he and his work together form a continuous link with the forces which will be summoned in the final ceremony when the sculpture is worn or carried by the dancer. The masked dancer and the drummers can communicate with the gods through their various arts, and are respected by the community for this power. They have been chosen as channels of communication by the gods, and their fame for their ability to use the power of the gods may spread many miles beyond their own territory.

The identity of the individual African sculptor has tended to become obscured, because he is manipulating forces which exist outside himself, so that once he has caused those forces to enter into the sculpture, he sinks into anonymity.

In a symposium called *The Artist in Tribal Society* Paul Bohannan, a social anthropologist who has made a study of the Tiv people in Nigeria, pointed out that a Tiv work of art is the product, not of the community but of God. The word for working in wood is *gba* and the only other use of this word refers to God's creation of the world. A craftsman will say of his work, 'it did not come out too badly' or 'it came out well', as if the process were completely independent of him. Bohannan concluded that Tiv people are interested in the art, not in the artist. He describes how he tried to make some chairs and stools himself with an adze and how as soon as he put the adze down someone would pick it up and work on the stool himself. He writes: 'I had a hand in all of them, but they are not my handiwork – the whole compound and half the countryside worked on them.'

Commenting on Bohannan's paper K. C. Murray, of the Nigerian Antiquities Department, described how Fanti fishermen from Ghana behaved in exactly the same way when they were decorating their boats. They are 'assisted by anyone who cares to join in and conform, usually to some general plan of decoration.' Murray points out that among some African people, the Fanti, the Tiv and the Ibo, art is essentially non-professional, but that among the Yoruba, Beni, or the Awka Ibo, specialisation has developed more thoroughly; carvers are guild or family organisations with established forms of apprenticeship. In *Arrow of God* Chinua Achebe the Nigerian novelist, an Ibo from Eastern Nigeria, describes a 'non-professional' carver at work:

Ezeulu's first son, Edogo, had left home early that day to finish the mask he was carving for a new ancestral spirit. It was now only five days to the Festival of the Pumpkin Leaves when this spirit was expected to return from the depths of the earth and appear to men as a Mask. Those who would act as his attendants were making great plans for his coming; they had learnt their dance and were now anxious about the mask Edogo was carving for them. There were other carvers in Umuaro besides him; some of them were even better. But Edogo had a reputation for finishing his work on time unlike Obiako, the master carver. who only took up his tools

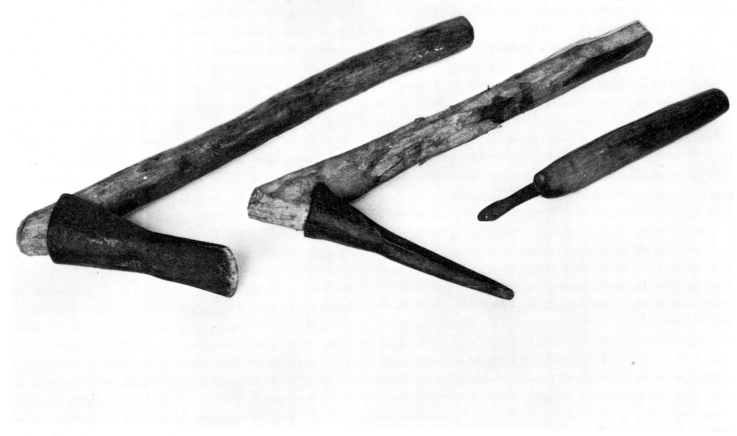

3. Woodcarver's tools. West Africa. British Museum, London.

when he saw his customers coming. If it had been any other kind of carving Edogo would have finished it long ago, working at it any moment his hands were free. But a mask was different; he could not do it in the home under the profane gaze of women and children but had to retire to the spirit-house built for such work at a secluded corner of the Nkwo market place. No one who had not been initiated into the secret of Masks would dare to approach the hut which faced the forest, away from the market place. At certain times when women were called upon to rub its red-earth exterior and decorate it with white, green, yellow and black patterns men were always there guarding the entrance.

The hut was dark inside although the eye got used to it after a short while. Edogo put down the white okwe wood on which he was going to work and then unslung his goat-skin bag in which he carried his tools. Apart from the need for secrecy, Edogo had always found the atmosphere of this hut right for carving masks. All around him were older masks and other regalia of ancestral spirits, some of them older than even his father. They produced a certain ambience which gave power and cunning to his fingers. Most of the masks were for fierce, aggressive spirits with horns and teeth the size of fingers. But four of them belonged to maiden-spirits and were delicately beautiful. Edogo remembered with a smile what Nwanyinma told him when he first married his wife. Nwanyinma was a widow with whom he had made friends in his bachelor days. In her jealousy against the younger rival she had told Edogo that only the woman whose breasts stayed erect year after year was the maiden-spirit.

Edogo sat down on the floor near the entrance where there was the most light and began to work. Now and again he heard the voices of people passing through the market place from one village of Umuaro to another. But when his carving finally got hold of him he heard no more voices.

THE MASQUERADE OF THE CULTS

It would not be a correct interpretation of African religious ceremonies if we made the same distinctions between the sacred and the profane as those which exist in European societies. It would be more accurate to regard the gods as the play-fellows of the ancestors and of the people living in the lineage group. The religious ceremonies often take the form of plays which go on for several days, and which are recast to amuse and entertain as well as to provide the mounting psychological tension which occurs before a sacrifice. In consequence a particular play may be adopted by another group of people as much as a hundred miles away, in the same way that masks or sculptures may be imported. The pantheons of African religions are like a collection of characters in a play, and a new god may be adopted

not only because he is thought to be powerful but because he is entertaining. Someone has witnessed his presence in someone else's pantheon and imported him into the new area. It may be that he is more terrifying or that he is more laughable. The two emotions are not easy to distinguish in many cases. Sometimes the dancers and the drummers will come and teach the people who have adopted the new god the particular rhythms and dance steps which go with it; and for this they will receive a fee. This process has been particularly well described by Robin Horton in an article, *The Kalabari Ekine Society; a Borderland of Religion and Art*, published in *Africa*. In this cult, a particular set of spirits have become more concerned with entertainment than with religious activities, although the link with the traditional religion is still very strong. The Kalabari Ijo live in the delta area of Nigeria. The Ekine spirits are water spirits as are most of the cult gods of the Ijo. They are invoked during the dry season of the year to come and 'walk with' the masqueraders who perform in a cycle of thirty to fifty masquerade plays. Horton says that these spirits are invoked not to grant 'general benefits, such as health, wealth, plentiful issue, and peace', but with the sole aim of ensuring the success of the play; 'the masquerade is not a means of getting something out of the gods; it is an end in itself'. The spirits invoked are those which live beyond the domains of the community and are outside the normal range of communal activity. They are 'not only unimportant in practical terms: they are actually dangerous'. Thus the myths of masquerade spirits like Egbelegbe and Agiri tell how, before these spirits were taken up by their present hosts, a succession of other communities had got rid of them after finding them dangerous to their players and insatiable in their demands for human sacrifices. Only the present hosts, so the myths go, were brave enough to ignore the danger and persevere enough to make these spirits accept animals rather than human beings as their food.

The more dangerous spirits are only used in the masquerades by the Ekine society proper, but a boy joins the junior society at the age of fifteen and the plays of this society are performed in the intervals between the Ekine society masquerade cycles. The preliminary offerings and invocations are an extremely important part of the Ekine masquerade, but the junior society does not encourage the presence of the spirits by making the offerings and invocations. Next, if the boy is particularly promising, he joins the junior grade of the society and his entry may be sponsored by a senior member who has spotted him. After this he goes through a test of recognising the dance rhythms of the ancestors by dancing them while pointing to the shrine of the ancestors for whom they are danced. When he has passed this test he pays sums of money to join various clubs in the senior grade, each of which holds the right to perform a particular play. These plays may be brought in by a member of the society who has seen them in some other village or town and has paid for the 'copyright'. Alternatively 'the water spirits' may come to him in a dream and teach him a new play. He may be remembered when he dies by an outstanding play that he purchased or composed from a vision, or he may be remembered by his aptitude as a dancer in a particular mask of the play. A miniature replica of his mask will be placed on his ancestor memorial and his heirs will inherit the right to dance in that mask or a whole play that he introduced.

Membership of the Ekine society has nothing to do with the political status of an individual. In fact success in the Ekine plays is quite independent of communal life in general. Heads of the Ekine society are not usually heads of town or village or prominent in their affairs. They are usually people who enjoy dancing and entertainment. However it is not considered acceptable in the community to avoid joining the Ekine society; a man who does not join is suspect, or thought of as someone who is too busy plotting the downfall of his opponents to join in the communities' means of entertainment.

In some cults a particular group of masqueraders will be more concerned with entertainment than other members of the cult. This has happened in the Egungun cult of the Yoruba in Nigeria. This is the Yoruba cult which is particularly concerned with the worship of ancestors. It is described by Ulli Beier in his book, *A Year of Sacred Festivals in One Small Yoruba Town*. A man will be told by the Ifa priest that his ancestor has been singled out for special worship and then he must have a mask made. The hereditary chief of the Egungun secret society then chooses a man to wear

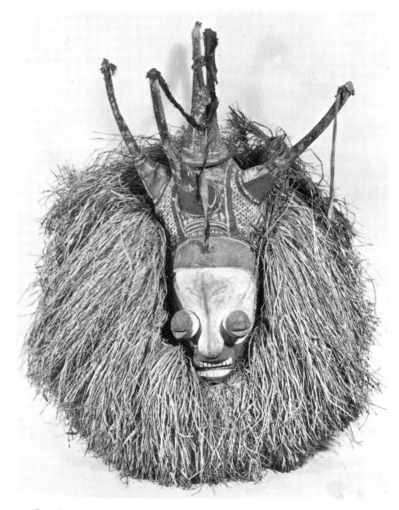

4. Bayaka mask. South Congo-Kinshasa. Wood and raffia. Height 25 in. (63.5 cm.). British Museum, London.

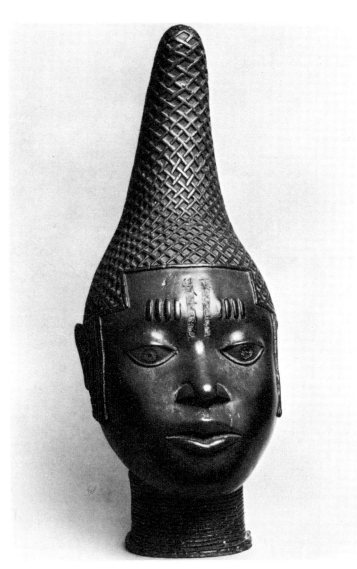

5. Head of a queen mother (Iyobu). Benin, southern Nigeria. Bronze. Height 15½ in. (39.4 cm.). British Museum, London.

the mask. When he is wearing the mask he may become possessed; then he ceases to speak with his normal voice, but is supposed to speak with the voice of the spirit of the ancestor whose mask it is. It is dangerous to come near these masks and at the ceremony men with sticks keep the crowds of people away. In the old days anyone who saw the face or even a part of the body of the masquerader was punished by death, and any woman who entered the area where a ceremony was being carried out would suffer a similar fate. One of the masks was called Gbajero, 'the hanger of witches', and was responsible for executing those who practised 'black magic'. In the past powerful Egungun would try to avoid each other, but if they met by accident they would fight for supremacy. One might try to hypnotise the other by commanding him to remain rooted to the ground, or dare the other to pick up a magic ring. The opponent knew that if he did not have the antidote to hand he would be struck by a terrible disease. One Egungun is supposed to have carried a swarm of bees on his mask to attack the opponent and return to the owner at his order.

Egungun of the entertainer branch of the secret society are called Agbe Igi Jo and they appear in plays in the market place. They may travel from town to town performing their plays which contain satirical figures, policemen, prostitutes, a local chief who is the subject of ridicule, and foreigners such as Europeans or Northern Nigerians. In the 1961 Federal Elections some of the masqueraders represented the various opposition parties which were organised on a regional basis.

Chinua Achebe has described similar secret societies devoted to ancestors by his own people, the Ibo. The ancestral spirits are called in to advise on the affairs of the community. They are regarded by the people of the village with affection, amusement and awe:

An iron gong sounded, setting up a wave of expectation in the crowd. Everyone looked in the direction of the egwugwu house. Gome, gome, gome, gome went the gong, and a powerful flute blew a high-pitched blast. Then came the voices of the egwugwu, guttural and awesome. The wave struck the women and children and there was a backward stampede. But it was momentary. They were already far enough where they stood and there was room for running away if any of the egwugwu should go towards them.

The drum sounded again and the flute blew. The egwugwu house was now a pandemonium of quavering voices: Aru oyim de de de de dei! filled the air as the spirits of the ancestors, just emerged from the earth, greeted themselves in their esoteric language. The egwugwu house into which they emerged faced the forest, away from the crowd, who saw only its back with the many-coloured patterns and drawings done by specially chosen women at regular intervals. These women never saw the inside of the hut. No woman ever did. They scrubbed and painted the outside walls under the supervision of men. If they imagined what was inside, they kept their imagination to themselves. No woman ever asked questions about the most powerful and the most secret cult in the clan.

Aru oyim de de de dei! flew around the dark, closed hut like tongues of fire. The ancestral spirits of the clan were abroad. The metal gong beat continuously now and the flute, shrill and powerful, floated on the chaos. And then the egwugwu appeared. The women and children sent up a great shout and took to their heels. It was instinctive. A woman fled as soon as an egwugwu came in sight. And when, as on that day, nine of the greatest masked spirits in the clan came out together it was a terrifying spectacle. Even Mgbafo took to her heels and had to be restrained by her brothers.

Each of the nine egwugwu represented a village of the clan. Their leader was called Evil Forest. Smoke poured out of his head.

The nine villages of Umuofia had grown out of the nine sons of the first father of the clan. Evil Forest represented the village of Umueru, or the children of Eruo, who was the eldest of the nine sons.

'Umuofia kwenu!' shouted the leading egwugwu, pushing the air with his raffia arms. The elders of the clan replied, 'Yaa!' 'Umuofia kwenu!' 'Yaa!' 'Umuofia kwenu!' 'Yaa!'.

Evil Forest then thrust the pointed end of his rattling staff into the earth. And it began to shake and rattle, like something agitating with a metallic life. He took the first of the empty stools and the eight other egwugwu began to sit in order of seniority after him.

The secret societies which are concerned more with pure entertainment than with religion, like the Ekine society of the Ijo described by Horton and the Agbe Igi Jo branch of Egungun masqueraders of the Yoruba, may at the same time have a more direct bearing on the ethics and ideals of the community. Horton, in an article in *Nigeria* magazine, has described how the Ekine masqueraders stage a graduation ceremony. If a new member fails to carry out the steps correctly then his mask will be taken from him by a rival house of masqueraders; those who have failed in this way have been known in the past to commit suicide. While the masquerader is listening for the drum calls which signal to him that he must perform a certain dance he must affect the utmost nonchalance. He must drink and flirt with the women and pretend that he is not listening to the drummer. Meanwhile the drummer will attempt to disguise the fact that he is making the calls by obscuring them in the general rhythms that he is playing. As soon as the call starts, however, the masquerader who is otherwise occupied, must respond with the correct salute to the ancestors. This nonchalance, which is expected from the dancer with the mask, symbolises the attitude which an Ijo man is supposed to have towards life. He must be capable of carrying out all his responsibilities to his kinsfolk while at the same time living life with great zest and without undue seriousness.

The entertainment masquerade therefore also reflects the way in which life is regulated in the society even if it has no direct concern with the affairs of that society. How does the mask itself affect the masquerade? Horton points out that the mask establishes the presence of the spirit. It is because of the presence of the mask that the dancer becomes possessed by the spirit owner of the play. However, the mask is not there to impress the spectators. Very often its features face the sky or are entirely enclosed in 'decoration' and are invisible from any angle. It is the dancer who is the most important feature in the masquerade. The plots of the plays are sketchy and the dominant symbols are those of rhythmic gesture, dictated by the drum. Apart from the preliminary offerings and invocations which are crucial, the important characteristics of a good masquerade are a good orchestra of drums and a dancer who can translate the drum rhythms smoothly into the gestures of the dance.

Perhaps this explains why the expression of a mask has a certain inwardness. It is the seat of the spirit who is 'riding' the dancer, to use the language of Haitian voodoo, but the spirit is actually expressing his personality through the dance, guided by the drum. The spirit is in the mask and the mask looks as if it is restraining an intense force within itself. The sculptors succeed in giving to the wood this sense of a power trying to burst out, a feeling of force concentrated within. It is only in the dancers' rhythms and gestures that the crowd actually watch the expression taking place, and the unleashing of the power of the spirit. Very often in the masquerades, for example in the Cameroun, the masked

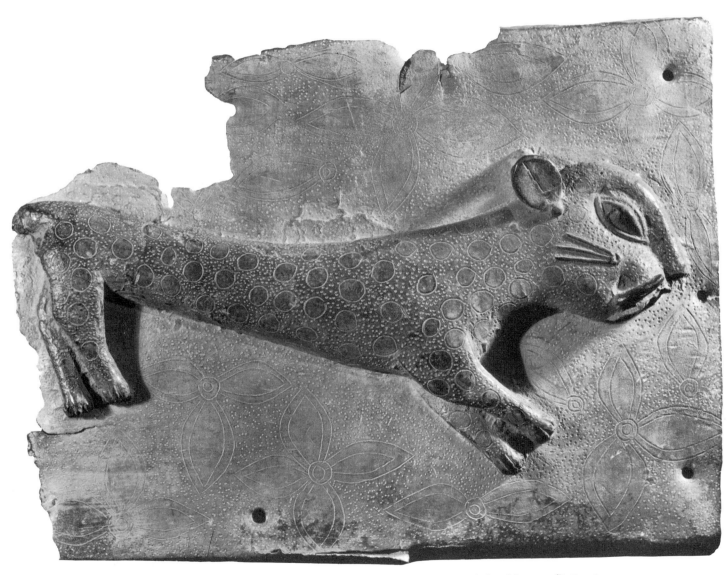

6. Bronze plaque with leopard. Benin, southern Nigeria. 12 × 15½ in. (30.5 × 39.4 cm.). Linden Museum, Stuttgart.

figures are held by ropes, keepers holding on to the ropes. If the spirit were to break loose it would be to the great danger of the spectators. The masked dancer tugs and strains at his leash and the keepers show the great effort with which they have to keep him under control. Horton tells us that the spirits are the material with which the masqueraders have to work, to subdue and mould to their will in the artistic creation of the entertainment.

SURREALISM AND AFRICAN ART

... I knew that one day I must leave the village, the farming, the hunting, and the swimming, to learn to read and write in the schools of which people never ceased to talk.
Thanks to my good memory I never lost sight of this objective. But the many other interests I used to have when I was a village child seem lost now. I can only recollect my wild dreams. I was a dreamy child brought up on ghost stories and the innumerable deities which peopled our world.

This is a quotation from *The Catechist* by J. W. Abruquah who is Ghanaian. They might serve as a commentary on much that is best in modern African painting and sculpture. A great deal has been written about how the modern African artist cannot continue in the great traditions of the past, because he no longer works within the religious framework of the traditional society. I have tried to show how a great deal of what has been labelled religion in the old African society was very often a question of art for its own sake. We must be aware that when we look at an African mask we may be looking at something intended more as a vehicle for entertainment than for an act of worship. However, I have also shown that there was a belief that the spirits themselves came and helped in that entertainment. The modern African artist who cannot produce work in the ancient tradition has merely lost the knowledge of how to control the spirits and put them to artistic use, because he has not been trained by the same masters as the traditional artist. Many modern African artists have assumed that they could emulate the traditional African artist by copying the external forms of the old masks and figures. This is merely reminiscent of a dead classicism, resulting in work without any vitality.

In the Surrealist language of artists like Paul Klee, this was what the masquerader was trying to achieve by summoning the spirits. He wanted his work of art to have 'a life of its own'. The difference between the two ways of speaking is the difference between regarding the work as originating in the human mind and becoming externalised as a dance or a gesture, or as being produced by some being from another world. The modern European artist makes associations which surprise him and of which he was not previously aware. It is the element of surprise which gives these associations the appearance of acting for themselves, of being outside his control, achieving a certain organic unity which causes the European artist to compare them to independent forms of life. The African in traditional society believed that there were personalities in things, in the world around him, which could behave in surprising and unpredictable ways. To make them behave a little more predictably was to produce a work of art.

The world of the spirits has been described by Amos Tutuola who draws on African folk stories. Here he describes the Satyr in his novel *Simbi and the Satyr of the Dark Jungle*:

When he approached them, they noticed that he did not wear neither coat nor trousers but he wore only an apron which was soaked with blood. Plenty of the soft feathers were stuck onto this apron. More than one thousand heads of birds were stuck to all over it. He was about ten feet tall and very strong, bold and vigorous. His head was full of dirty long hairs and the hairs were full up with refuses and dried leaves. The mouth was so large and wide that it almost covered the nose. The eyes were so fearful that a person could not be able to look at them for two times, especially the powerful illumination they were bringing out always. He wore plenty of juju-beads round his neck. The spider's webs were spread over his mouth and this showed that he had not eaten for a long time. This Satyr was a pessimist, he was impatient and ill-tempered, impenitent and noxious creature. His beard was so long and bushy that it was touching the ground and he was using it for sweeping his house as if it was a broom. In respect of all these things, the king of this Dark Jungle appointed him as the guard of the jungle, and this Dark Jungle itself was the home of imps, gnomes, goblins and all other kinds of evil spirits and there was a bold phoenix which was always flying to everywhere in this jungle, it was swallowing all kinds of other creatures which were coming there. And it was also appointed by the king to be an assistance for the Satyr.
This Satyr was always with a bunch of cudgels on head and one club of bone in hand. He was all the time carrying all these things about in the jungle.

AFRICAN ART TODAY

It is sometimes suggested that the modern African artist has not carried on the traditions of his great predecessors because he has been the victim of colonialism or conversion to Christianity, or that latterly tourists have encouraged the production of cheap imitations of the old carvings, known as 'airport art'. This is partly true but the demand that the modern African artist should live up to his past imposes a considerable burden upon him. Very often he is conscious that he must make a break with the past, if studying the past means too great a concern for outmoded forms of expression. The modern African artists who have succeeded are not bemused by the external appearance of the old African sculpture, but recognise that the forces straining to break out of the traditional mask into dance or poetry can also be found within themselves, and can be made to assist them in producing completely new forms of expression in modern painting and sculpture. I have chosen the illustrations of modern African art to show the work of artists who have never left their native country or been to art school, of those who have worked in art schools and studios in Africa, and of those who have been to art schools and have worked in cities outside Africa such as London and Paris.

It is interesting to consider the number of European painters who have collected African art and who have been influenced by it. Some have lived in Africa and have run art schools and academies there. One of the first was K. C. Murray who began to teach painting at Omu-Aran in Northern Nigeria in 1928 and who laid the foundation of the Department of Antiquities in Nigeria. He collected a vast quantity of works of Nigerian art and then persuaded the Nigerian government to build a museum to house them in Lagos. In 1941 Meyerowitz started an Arts Institute at Achimota in Ghana, and invited a number of artists to join him, including Michael Cardew the potter. Cardew stayed in West Africa until 1966 and built two potteries, one at Vume in Ghana and another at Abuja in Northern Nigeria where he taught traditional potters to use the wheel and to make high temperature glazes. Three of the most recent additions to this list are Ulli Beier, Frank MacEwen and Julian Beinart. Ulli Beier went to Nigeria in 1951 and in 1953 he

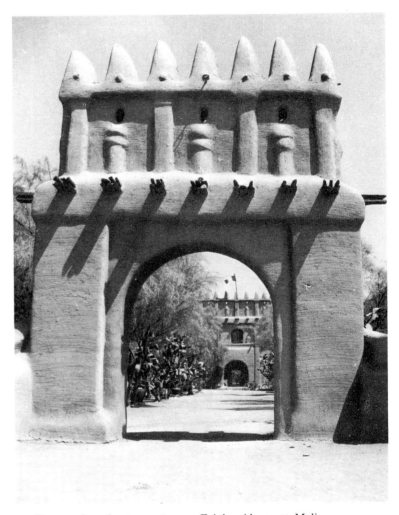

7. Decorated mud gateway to an official residence at Mali.

started the magazine *Black Orpheus* with the help of the Western Nigeria Literature Agency. This magazine was intended to increase an awareness of African and Afro-American literature, but from the beginning it also included reproductions of the work of African artists such as Ibrahim Salahi, Malangatana Valente and Asiru (plates 46, 44, 50).

In 1961 Ulli Beier initiated the Mbari Artists and Writers Centre in Ibadan with the assistance of the Extra-Mural Department of the University of Ibadan. The walls were decorated by Nigerian artists. Exhibitions were held there and art workshops set up. Later he started Mbari centres in Oshogbo and in Lagos. His collaborators in these projects were the Nigerian writers Wole Soyinka, Chinua Achebe, Christopher Okigbo, J. P. Clark, and the stage designer, Demas Nwoko. In Oshogbo Ulli Beier worked closely with the Austrian artist, Susanne Wenger, who decorated many of the old buildings and shrines with her own cement sculpture and wood screens. Susanne Wenger helped sculptors such as Asiru who was originally making small pieces of jewellry and ornaments for sale. She and Ulli Beier encouraged Asiru to work on the large sheets of aluminium he uses now. The Dutch graphic artist, Van Rossem, went to Oshogbo and ran a summer school in etching. After he left, Ulli Beier's wife, Georgina, started a studio together with a gallery of popular art, folk art and modern African paintings and sculpture which Ulli Beier had made there. The Mbari Mbayo club of Oshogbo, Van Rossem's summer school and Georgina Beier's studio all helped to produce artists such as Twins Seven Seven (plate 49). He is one of a group of Oshogbo artists including Asiru, Yemi Bisiri, Murainoa Cyelami, Jacob Afolabi and Rufus Ogundele who exhibited at the Institute of Contemporary Arts in London in March 1967, and whose work has also been exhibited in Amsterdam, Munich and Berlin.

Julian Beinart, who is at present Professor of Town Planning in the University of Cape Town, South Africa, started his summer schools at the Mbari centres in Ibadan and Oshogbo. The first one was held in 1962. Since then he has held them in South Africa, in Zambia and in Kenya. The object is to bring together practising artists and people who may never have painted before. Beinart encourages them to use all kinds of materials, housepaint, feathers, matches,

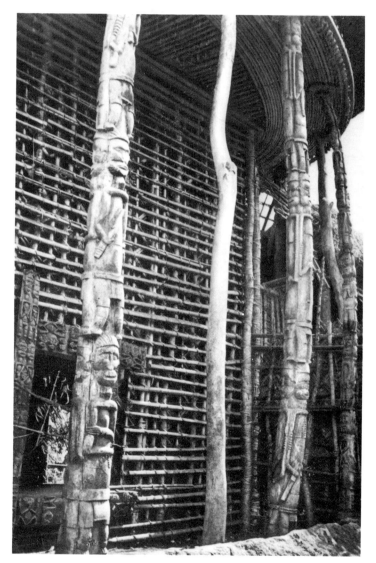

8. Wall of the Bamileke Palace, Cameroun.

bottle-tops, medicinal lozenges, pieces of chalk, and to build them into exciting collages. In this way he hopes to get away from the kind of art school image which has been imposed on the painter in Africa, where nineteenth century academic art has flourished long after its demise in Europe; and where traditional African art has been used to institute a new academicism. The modern art of Africa may not be like anything Africa has known before, but Beinart thinks it may spring up in the new towns. He has collected hundreds of drawings and photographs of wall paintings and exteriors in Western Native Township, Johannesburg, before they were demolished, and has joined with Ulli Beier in collecting photographs of the popular art of the Mbari areas of Africa such as barber's signs and cinema posters.

A few years ago Frank MacEwen tried a similar experiment in the painting workshops of the Rhodesian National Gallery in Salisbury. The paintings of the gallery caretaker, Thomas Mukarobgwa, have become widely known and have been bought by the Museum of Modern Art in New York. Bricklayers, jazz musicians and witch doctors have done similar work. The best of this is some very powerful stone carvings strongly reminiscent of masks from the area of the Southern Bantu (see map on page 31).

A Portuguese architect of international reputation, Amancio D'Alpoim Guedes, has started a workshop in his own compound in Lourenco Marques. It was he who discovered Malangatana Valente working as a boy picking up tennis balls at the club and who encouraged him to paint. Guedes has since used a lot of the painting and sculpture from his workshop in his own buildings.

The modern painters of Africa are becoming independent of the past. The French-speaking African painters have been most aware of the past but as a vague, romantic image, and so far it would be true to say that they have not produced any very original talent. It is the painters who have been farthest away from the centres of African traditional art, the painters of the Sudan and of Ethiopia, who have carried modern African art furthest into the future.

Ibrahim Salahi, head of the School of Fine Art in the University of Khartoum in the Sudanese Republic, has told us a great deal about his manner of working in an interview published in the newsletter of the Transcription Centre in

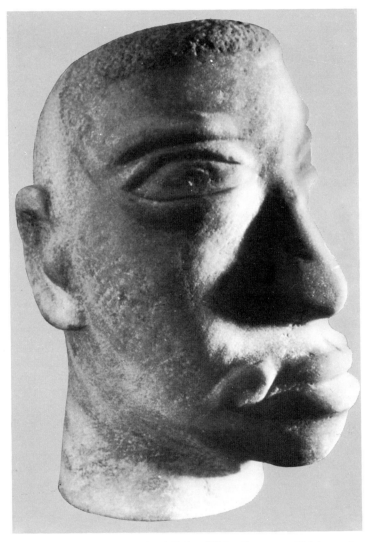

9. Head of a man by Tubayi Dube. White limestone. Height 14 in. (35.5 cm.). Rhodes National Gallery, Salisbury.

London, *Cultural Events in Africa* for February 1967. He was talking to Robert Serumaga, a Ugandan writer, who asked him whether he had gained anything from studying at the Slade School of Art in London. Salahi replied that the knowledge and experience he gained there did not help him to express himself in his own way. He went on to describe how he himself worked:

I find when I am working certain words come to me. I usually feel nervous, almost like a chicken trying to lay an egg, when I have an idea. And then suddenly I have words that come to me; then I start chasing them, I start repeating them, humming, and then sometimes some of them appear on the work itself. I find I've done them without realising it. Their meaning is prayer mostly. Some of it is poetry; some of it is directly from the Koran, and some of it is just things which come into my head which have no meaning at all, just words put together. And they seem to come through me and appear on the canvas.

It is interesting to compare what Salahi says, with the words of a poet, Christopher Okigbo, who died in 1967 fighting for Biafra. In another of Robert Serumaga's conversations with African writers and artists (July 1965), which are to be published in a collection by Heinemann, he claimed that he did not write his poem, *Lament of the Drums*:

All I did was to create the drums, and the drums said what they liked. Personally I don't believe that I am capable of saying what the drums have said. It's only the long funeral drums that are capable of saying it, and they are capable of saying it only at that moment. So I don't think I can claim to have written the poem; all I did was to cover the drums, and to create the situation in which the drums spoke what they spoke.

The main sources of Salahi's and Okigbo's work then, despite their use of very new means of expression, are firmly rooted in their backgrounds, in Salahi's case, in the Islamic religion, in Okigbo's case in the ancestral drum rhythms. Okigbo went on to say:

I think all we hear nowadays of men-of-two-worlds is a lot of nonsense. I belong, integrally, to my own society, just as, I believe, I belong also integrally to other societies than my own. The truth is that the modern African is no longer a product of an entirely indigenous culture. The modern sensibility, which the modern African poet is trying to express, is by its very nature complex;

and it has complex values, some of which are indigenous, some exotic, some traditional, some modern. Some of these values are Christian, some non-Christian, and I think that anybody who thinks it is possible to express consistently only one line of values, indigenous or exotic, is probably being artificial.

Paul Klee and Wilfredo Lam seem to be strong influences in the work of Salahi, Max Ernst and Wols in the work of Skunder, but it is important for them both and for most modern African artists that they should be receptive to environmental influences. The landscape and the decorative architecture of Ethiopia seem to be present in Skunder's painting as well as the forms of modern biological science. Very often they are divided into separate areas of action like old Coptic paintings. Perhaps Surrealism is held in such esteem by these African painters because it is a method of giving the environmental forces that have played an important role in their development a chance to take over and control the means of expression at their disposal.

SELECTED BOOK LIST

Traditional and historical African art

African Design. Margaret Trowell. Faber, London 1960

Afrikanische Plastik. J. Sydow. Gebr. Mann, Berlin 1954

The Art of the Negro Peoples. E. Leuzinger. Methuen, London 1960

The Artist in Tribal Society. Proceedings of a Symposium held at the Royal Anthropological Institute. Marion Smith (Editor). Routledge and Kegan Paul, London 1961

Les Arts Plastiques du Congo Belge. Translated by M. Olbrechts. Edition Erasma, S A, Brussels 1959

Centres de Style de la Sculpture Nègre Africaine. Carl Kjersmeier, Editions Albert Morancé, Paris 1935-38

Les Bamiléké, Une Civilisation Africaine. Raymond Lecoq. Présence Africaine. Paris 1953.

Handbuch der Afrikanischen Plastik. J. Sydow. O. Reimer, Berlin 1939

Ife in the History of West African Sculpture. Frank Willett. Thames and Hudson, London 1967

Kalabari Sculpture. Robin Horton. Department of Antiquities, Nigeria 1965

Nigerian Art. Ulli Beier, Cambridge University Press 1960.

Nigerian Images. William Fagg. Lund Humphries, London 1963

The Sculpture of Africa. Eliot Elisofon and William Fagg. Thames and Hudson, London 1958

A Year of Sacred Festivals in One Small Yoruba Town. Ulli Beier.

Five Plays. Wole Soyinka. Oxford University Press, London 1964

My Life in the Bush of Ghosts. Amos Tutuola. Faber, London 1954

The Palm-Wine Drinkard. Amos Tutuola. Faber, London 1952

Simbi and the Satyr of the Dark Jungle. Amos Tutuola. Faber, London 1955

Things Fall Apart. Chinua Achebe. Heinemann, London 1958

Three Plays. J. P. Clark. Oxford University Press, London 1964

Philosophy

Bantu Philosophy. Father Placide Tempels. Présence Africaine, Paris 1953

The Mind of Africa. William Abraham. Weidenfeld and Nicolson, London 1962

Ethnology

Africa. Its Peoples and their Cultural History. G. P. Murdock. MacGraw-Hill, New York and London 1959

African Worlds. Daryll Forde (Editor). Published for the International African Institute by Oxford University Press, London 1954

A Borderland of Religion and Art. The Kalabari Ekine Society. Article in Africa. Volume 33, No. 2. Journal of the International African Institute. Oxford University Press, London 1963

The Gods as Guests. Robin Horton. Nigeria Magazine, Lagos 1960

Igbo Village Affairs. Margaret Green. Cass, London 1947

Les Peuples et les Civilisations de l'Afrique. H. Baumann and D. Westermann. Payot, Paris 1948

Notes on the map

The ethnographical divisions are based on those given by G. P. Murdock in his book, *Africa, its Peoples and their Cultural History*. Slight amendments have been made to Murdock's divisions, however, as he considers types of African culture mainly in relation to differences in agriculture and in social structure. In this book, religion is considered a more important factor in distinguishing one form of art from another. Certain exceptions will be found to this scheme, because there is not always a consistency in religion, language and artistic style between tribes, or between the smaller social groupings within a tribe. This may be due to conquests and immigrations, enforced or peaceful, which have occurred every few years over most of the area we are dealing with. Sometimes it is simply a result of borrowing between tribes as explained in the introduction.

It is possible to construct a very general framework of religious behaviour for each of the areas shown on the map, and to distinguish each area by one main element which is emphasised more than others by the peoples who live in that area.

The Mongo peoples are an exception. Here there is a great diversity of religious behaviour and the distinguishing characteristic is artistic rather than religious (see plate 16). They have preserved some of the art of the Savannah, their masks and figures being more ordered and geometrical. The Mongo are Equatorial Bantu and have pushed across the Congo river and settled in the bend of the Congo and the Kasai, its southern tributary.

The Mande group, called after the main language group in their area, which includes the Bambara (plate 11) and the Marka (plate 25), are very much aware of order in their universe and emphasise numbers and topological patterns when describing it.

The Kru and Coastal Mande, which include the Toma (plate 9), have very powerful secret societies which enforce strong moral prescriptions and sanctions in their communities, in order to keep the community together.

The Voltaic peoples, which include the Dogon (plate 22), the Bobo-Fing (plate 1) and the Kurumba (plate 2), emphasise strongly the earth deity in their religion.

The Akan peoples, which include the Atye (plate 10) and the Ashanti (plate 37), have a pantheon of deities of earth and sky, rivers and mountains, but emphasise those particular cults which are associated with their chiefs and the personalities of their chiefs.

The Kwa peoples, which include the Fon of Dahomey (plate 21), the Yoruba (plates 29, 30, 32, 33, 34, 35), the Ibo (plate 3) and the Kalabari Ijo (plate 39), have a pantheon of deities, but (apart from the Fon of Dahomey, who appear to have a monolithic social structure), these peoples have divisive social structures, with differing cults adopted by the various contending interests and parties in the communities.

The North Western Bantu, which include the Bakwele (plate 15) and the Bateke (plate 6), emphasise their ancestors in secret societies. These societies are also very individualistic and divided, and the men's and women's societies and the societies of various kin groups and age groups exist in rivalry with one another. There are societies which enforce law and order, but they are not so powerful as the Poro society of the Mande and the other secret societies of the coastal Mande and Kwa peoples.

The peoples of the Cameroon highlands, the Bamum, Bafo (plates 5 and 14), and Bamileke (plates 18, 19 and 20) are divided into a number of smaller groups which have extraordinarily large rulers' courts in comparison to their size. The Bamileke have ninety chiefdoms of which the largest contains approximately 27,000 people, and the smallest five hundred people. The chiefs live in big houses almost like palaces with a great display of decoration and sculpture, while their people live scattered in small hamlets all over the countryside. The societies through which the chief establishes law and order are not so secretive as those of other ethnic groups which have been discussed, but often operate in daylight with a dazzling display of colour in their masks and costumes. The chiefs sit on elaborately carved and beaded thrones, and all the musical instruments and appurtenances of the ceremonies are carved and decorated in an almost baroque fashion. In these peoples it is as if the mysteries are operated openly and are much more connected with the materialistic success of the society.

The Equatorial Bantu, represented here by the Bakota (plate 13), consist of people who have moved southwards and westwards from the Savannah areas of Central Africa and pushed their way between the original Bantu inhabitants of the area (the North Western Bantu). Their religion is characterised by totemism, by the belief in reincarnation of animals in human beings, and by the transmutation into animals of those who die.

The Luba peoples, represented by the Lualwa, have powerful chiefs supported by a cult of ancestors. One people, the Baluba, have imposed their art styles on practically every ethnic group in the area.

The Southern Bantu, represented by the Bapende (plate 21), the Bayaka (plate 26), the Bakuba (plate 7) and the Basonge (plate 8), are found from the west coast of Central Africa to the East coast. Their religion is characterised by an emphasis on using the life-force in nature by means of divination, particularly in the making of rain. There is a widespread belief in the power of witchcraft and diviners are consulted in order to detect witches, who used to be tested by poison ordeal. The Basonge mask was used in a witch-hunting ceremony. The hunting of witches and sorcerers is supposed to help in the internal cohesion of a divided community.

Ethnographical map

KEY

Mande

Coastal Mande and Kru

Voltaic

Akan

Kwa

North Western Bantu

Cameroon Grasslands

Equatorial Bantu

Mongo

Luba

Southern Bantu

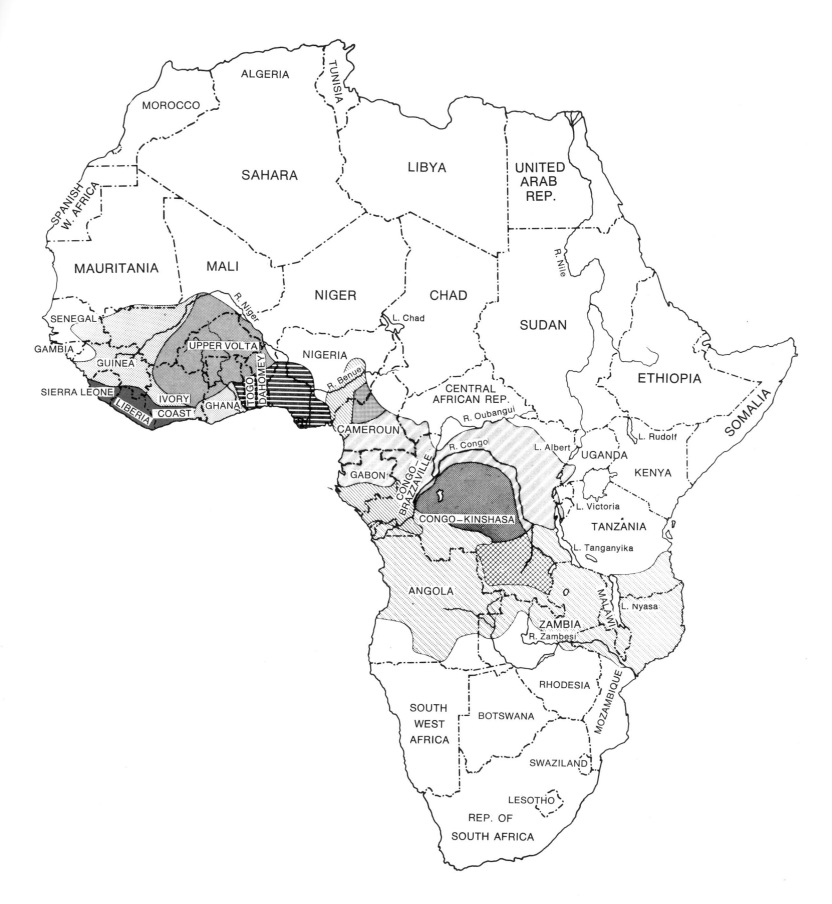

MOROCCO

ALGERIA

TUNISIA

LIBYA

UNITED
ARAB
REP.

SPANISH
W. AFRICA

SAHARA

MAURITANIA

MALI

NIGER

CHAD

SUDAN

ETHIOPIA

SENEGAL

R. Niger

R. Nile

GAMBIA

UPPER VOLTA

NIGERIA

SOMALIA

GUINEA

R. Benue

SIERRA LEONE

LIBERIA

IVORY
COAST

GHANA

TOGO

DAHOMEY

CAMEROUN

CENTRAL
AFRICAN REP.

R. Oubangui

L. Rudolf

R. Congo

L. Albert

UGANDA

GABON

CONGO-
BRAZZAVILLE

KENYA

CONGO—KINSHASA

L. Victoria

TANZANIA

L. Tanganyika

ANGOLA

MALAWI

L. Nyasa

ZAMBIA

R. Zambesi

RHODESIA

MOZAMBIQUE

SOUTH
WEST
AFRICA

BOTSWANA

SWAZILAND

LESOTHO

REP. OF
SOUTH AFRICA

Notes on the plates

Our approach to African art is very much dictated by the preoccupations of the art of our own times. Roger Fry wrote in 1910 in *Vision and Design*:

'the negro scores heavily by his willingness to reduce the limbs to a succession of ovoid masses sometimes scarcely longer than they are broad. Generally speaking, we may say that his plastic sense leads him to give the utmost amplitude and relief to all parts of the body, and to get thereby an extraordinarily emphatic and impressive sequence of planes. So far from clinging to two dimensions, as we tend to do, he actually underlines, as it were, the three-dimensionalness of his forms. It is in some such way, I suspect that he manages to give to his forms their disconcerting vitality, the suggestion that they make of being not mere echoes of actual figures, but of possessing an inner life of their own.'

Roger Fry was influenced in his approach to African art by the prevailing climate of Cubism, by Derain, Modigliani and Brancusi. He emphasised its three-dimensionality. Today with our experience of surrealism, pop art, op art and hard edge, we are more influenced by the polychrome qualities and the optical effects of African art. This has dictated the choice of illustrations in this book. The great historians of African art, Sydow, Kjersmeier, Olbrechts and William Fagg have emphasised the three-dimensional quality that Fry looked for. They seem to have concentrated on those masks and figures which showed the African sculptor's grasp of the roundness of forms and their resolution, and the happy combination of the sphere, the box and the cylinder. Perhaps it is time to turn the balance the other way and to look more closely at the African sculptor as painter as well as sculptor, at his juxtaposition of colour shapes and concave and convex surfaces to produce a psychic effect.

Plate 1 *Helmet mask of the Do Guardian Spirit* of the Bobo-Fing people living in the Bobo Djulasso area, Upper Volta. Height 15¼ in. (38 cm.). Rietberg Museum, Zurich.
In this Bobo-Fing mask the protuberant features of eyes, nose and mouth are left dark in contrast to the white surround. This helps to emphasise the shadows in the cavities and gives the whole mask an air of suffering from its experiences in the underworld.

Plate 2 *Kurumba Dancer's Mask*. Upper Volta. Wood. Height 27½ in. (69 cm.). Musée de l'Homme, Paris.

The Kurumba dancers of the Aribinda region of Upper Volta drive away the souls of the dead from the village during the period of mourning by wearing this mask. Here the geometrical pattern of colour imposed on a basic animal shape, in this case an antelope, creates the mystery.

Plate 3 *Nmwo Society Mask of the Ibo*. Eastern Nigeria. Wood. Height 17 in. (43 cm.). American Museum of Natural History, New York.
There are two types of spirits represented in the masks of this society, one female and one male. The female, represented here, is always painted white on top of a very delicate form, with a sensitive design in black picked out from the head-dress and the facial markings. Its effect in a carving is described in Chinua Achebe's novel, *Things Fall Apart* (see book list on page 32).

Plate 4 *Mask of the Ekpo Society of the Ibibio*. Eastern Nigeria. Wood. Height 12 in. (30 cm.). Linden Museum, Stuttgart.
This mask has a hinged jaw and is worn by members of the Ekpo secret society. This society is responsible for law and order in the community and may remove criminals in the night. Ibibio carving shows a great concern with the plastic effect of planes and cylinders, but the power of this mask is increased by the woven head-dress of straw. The Ibibio belong to the North Western Bantu peoples.

Plate 5 *Bamum Throne*. Cameroons. Height 32¾ in. (83 cm.). Museum für Völkerkunde, Berlin-Dahlem.
This is a chief's throne and shows the expression of his power in its elaborate decoration. Such thrones are carved and beaded, and all the musical instruments and appurtenances of the ceremonies are carved and decorated in an almost baroque fashion.

Plate 6 *Bateke Mask*. Congo. Wood. Height 13¾ in. (35 cm.). Musée de l'Homme, Paris.
The Bateke live on both sides of the Congo, partly in Congo-Brazzaville and partly in Congo-Kinshasa in the region of Stanley Pool, and belong to the North Western Bantu (see map page 31). There is only one good example of this mask and a number of inferior copies. It is remarkable how the

semi-circles representing the lower lids of the eyes are slightly off-set so that the top of the face and the eyes themselves appear to move forwards.

Plate 7 *Shene Malula Mask*. Central Congo. Wood. Height 9 in. (23 cm.). Von der Heydt Collection, Rietberg Museum, Zurich.
This Bakuba mask of the Babende society is an initiation mask for a society formed by the young men to carry out the orders of the chief. The band of bright beads closing the mouth and running down from the nose probably symbolises an oath of secrecy.

Plate 8 *Kalebue Mask*. Basonge, Congo-Kinshasa. Wood. Height 24⅞ in. (63 cm.). Pinto Collection, Paris.
The Basonge belong to the Southern Bantu (see map on page 31). This mask, which is the most outstanding example of this kind collected, shows how the Basonge sculptor thinks in lines rather than planes. The box-like eyes and mouth are chunky masses against an area of sweeping lines. This mask perhaps more than any other demonstrates the theatrical effect of African traditional sculpture.

Plate 9 *Toma Mask*. Guinea. Wood. Height 35½ in. (90 cm.). Collection of Mrs Peggy Guggenheim, Venice.
The Toma, who belong to the Coastal Mende and Kru area (see map), live in the interior of Guinea. This is a mask of a spirit of the bush used by the Poro Society. It shows the opposite principle to the Bobo Fing mask in plate 1. Here the whiteness of the eyes makes them recede in a totally dark mass, and the effect is one of confident severity.

Plate 10 *Atye Mask*. Ivory Coast. Wood. Height 11 in. (28 cm.). Collection of M. Charles Rattan, Paris.
The Atye belong to the Akan group. This mask has been coated with a thick substance to create a rough surface. This increases its effect of coming from another world, the world of the spirits concerned with the earth and the rocks and hills.

Plate 11 *Bambara Mask*. Mali. Wood. Height 25½ in. (65 cm.). Collection of M. Pierre Vérité, Paris.

The Bambara live in Mali and belong to the Mande group. This *ci wara* or antelope mask is worn on top of a large tent-like covering of straw, and the rhythm of the radiating spokes of the mask helps to accentuate the movement in the dance of bowing to the earth. This is a good example of the exponential curve (see Introduction).

Plate 12 *Urhobo Kneeling Figure*. Nigeria. Wood. Height 26⅛ in. (66.5 cm.). Museum of Primitive Art, New York.
The Urhobo, belonging to the Kwa group, live between the Bini and the Ijo in the Niger delta of Nigeria. They were once included in the empire of Benin and their sculpture is like that of Edo-speaking people, (generally the Edo-speakers were all part of the old Benin). It is strong and confident and has a marked four-sidedness, which is to say that the sculptor first squared the tree-trunk into a box-shape and carved out the figure from four separate sides.

Plate 13 *Bakota Funerary Figure*. Gabon. Brassplated. Height 26½ in. (68 cm.). British Museum, London.
The Bakota live in the south east of the Ogowe river in Gabon in the area of the North West Bantu (see map). The influence of their highly stylised abstract sculpture for protecting the souls of the dead can be seen in the early work of Picasso, for example in his *Dancer* of 1907.

Plate 14 *Bafo Mask*. Cameroons. Wood. Height 12½ in. (31.5 cm.). Museum für Völkerkunde, Berlin-Dahlem.
The Bafo belong to the Cameroon highlands. All the sculpture of this area seems to have an almost Art Nouveau line in that it is imposed on the three-dimensional form in such a way that it follows its own course and always completes the enclosure. Nevertheless it is intimately related to the surface of the mask or figure and produces an effective marriage between them.

Plate 15 *Bakwele Mask*. Congo-Brazzaville. Wood. Height 9⅜ in. (24 cm.). Collection of M. Christophe Tzara, Paris.
The Bakwele live in the interior of Congo-Brazzaville not far from the Congo river and belong to the North Western Bantu. Many of the masks of this area have a frontal appearance and rely on a two-dimensional effect. Here the

eyes are slightly out of alignment with the heart-shape of the face and seem to rotate on an axis created by the bar over the mouth.

Plate 16 *Ndengese Figure*. Wood. Height 26¾ in. (68 cm.). Ethnological Collection, Zurich University.
The Ndengese come from the Mongo area. The cylinder on the head is a receptacle for holding offerings to the spirit-force which works through the figure. This figure, like the Afo figure in plate 40, shows how the scarification used to make designs on human bodies (see plate 51) is also used with great effect in sculpture. The Ndengese have been influenced by the Baluba who live to the south of them, but the geometrical treatment of this figure shows the Savannah influence among the Mongo peoples.

Plate 17 *Baluba Figure*. Congo-Kinshasa. Wood. Height 21⅝ in. (55 cm.). British Museum, London.
The Baluba were masters of a vast empire in Central Africa in the 18th century. They imposed their art style on people of the surrounding areas, notably the very naturalistic figures with expressive concave surfaces and the limbs making dynamic gestures. The Baluba belong to the Luba group.

Plate 18 *Bacham Mask*. Cameroon Highlands. Wood. Height 26 in. (66 cm.). Rietberg Museum, Zurich.
The Bacham are a sub-group of the Bamileke (see map). This mask has something of the baroque character of conspicuous display, typical of the societies of rank which support the chief. The baroque quality is even more vividly displayed in plates 19 and 20.

Plate 19 *Bamileke Masquerader*. Cameroons. Beadwork sewn with raffia.
Masquerader wearing a costume and mask head-dress (see note on plate 18).

Plate 20 *Bamileke Masquerader*. Cameroons. Beadwork sewn with raffia.
Masquerader wearing costume and dance head-dress (see note on plate 18).

Plate 21 *Bapende Mask*. Congo-Kinshasa. Wood. Height 20¼ in. (51.5 cm.). British Museum, London.
The Bapende belong to the area of the Southern Bantu and live on the Kasai river in the south of Congo-Kinshasa. Their art is not so frontal and geometrical as that of the Bakwele and the Bateke of the North Western Bantu. Nevertheless the Bapende rely on simple geometrical forms, the heart for the face, the cylinders for the eyes, to create the effect of a spiritual force working through the figure. The same theatricality can be observed as in the Basonge mask (plate 8).

Plate 22 *Dogon Mask*. Upper Volta. Wood. Height 22 in. (55 cm.). British Museum, London.
The Dogon belong to the Voltaic peoples. Superficially it may appear that they love cosmological order as do the Bambara of the Mande group. What they seem to be emphasising, however, is the way in which man is poised between earth and sky, and the vertical-horizontal structures on the heads of their masks express this feeling.

Plate 23 *Yoruba Mask*. Dahomey. Wood. Height 14⅛ in. (36 cm.). Collection of E. Müller Solothurn, Zurich.
The Yoruba people spread across the border from Western Nigeria into Dahomey. The Gelede cult, which is particularly active in fighting witchcraft, is prevalent especially among the Yoruba in Dahomey. The Gelede society have a special kind of double-headed mask of which a remarkable feature is the earthy polychrome painting.

Plate 24 *Baule Mask*. Ivory Coast. Wood. Height 19¼ in. (50 cm.). Collection Eduard von der Heydt. Rietberg Museum, Zurich.
The Baule from the Ivory Coast belong to the Akan area. This mask, however, has a strong stylistic resemblance to their northern neighbours, the Senufo, who are in the Voltaic area.

Plate 25 *Marka Mask*. French Sudan. Wood partly covered with metal. Height 14⅛ in. (36 cm.). Ethnological Collection, Zurich University.
The Marka of Mali belong to the Mande group of peoples. Their masks, and those of other people in the same area,

are frequently covered with copper or other metals; so also is most of the sculpture, which is done by blacksmiths. This mask in particular shows the sense of a very detailed cosmology with rules about man's behaviour.

Plate 26 *Bayaka Mask*. Congo-Kinshasa. Wood and raffia. Height 21⅝ in. (55 cm.). Collection Eduard von der Heydt, Rietberg Museum, Zurich.
The Bayaka are in the Southern Bantu area south of Congo-Kinshasa. This mask shows again the strong tendency in this area towards creating a theatrical effect in their masks.

Plate 27 *Cave Painting, Tassili*. Algeria.
In this and the three succeeding plates we come to what should be called historical, as distinct from traditional, African art, which is dying out as pre-industrial society gives way to urbanisation and modern education. The oldest examples of historical African art are cave paintings such as this. Some may be two thousand years old, but others are probably fairly recent. They are often the scene of initiation ceremonies which are still enacted today in places considered sacred because of their antiquity.

Plate 28 *Ife Head*. Nigeria. Bronze. Height 4½ in. (11.5 cm.). Musée d'Ife, Nigeria.
Ife is the ancient burial ground of the kings of the old Yoruba empire of Ife in Nigeria. Some of the bronzes found there may be a thousand years old.

Plates 29a and b *Jema'a Head*. Nok, Nigeria. Terracotta. Height 15 in. (31 cm.). Pitt Rivers Museum, Oxford.
A great many terracotta heads and figures have been found in alluvial deposits by the mining firms on the Bauchi plateau in Northern Nigeria. Carbon dating shows these terracottas to be two thousand years old. There are remarkable similarities with the Ife heads made at least a thousand years later and three hundred miles to the south.

Plate 30 *Door-Post of Yoruba Chief's Palace*. Idanre, Western Nigeria. Wood. Height 70¼ in. (178 cm.). British Museum, London.
See note to plate 32.

Plate 31 *Benin Plaque*. Nigeria. Bronze. Height of central figure 17 in. (43 cm.). British Museum, London.
The rulers of Ife are believed to have created the Benin empire in the fifteenth century and to have introduced their bronze-casting methods, among them the lost-wax process.

Plate 32 *Yoruba Carved Door*. Nigeria. Wood. Height of central figure, lower panel 15 in. (38 cm.). British Museum, London.
The Yoruba of Western Nigeria, who belong in the Kwa group, are prolific carvers and their carving is used for every conceivable purpose. Some of it adorns public buildings as in this plate. Some is hidden away in shrines and seldom seen by anyone except priests (plate 35); some is brought out on special occasions as in the feast of images at Ilobu. (plates 33 and 34).

Plate 33 *Dancing in Yoruba Festival*. Yemoja Festival, Ibadan, Western Nigeria. See note to plate 32.

Plate 34 *Dancing in Yoruba Festival*. Festival of Images, Ilobu, Western Nigeria. See note to plate 32

Plate 35 *Yoruba shrine*. Ogiyan. Ibadan, Western Nigeria. See note to plate 32.

Plate 36 *Adinkra Cloth* (detail). Akan. Total size 12 ft. 4½ in. × 6 ft. 11⅞ in. (3.46 × 2.13 m.). Linden Museum, Stuttgart.
This is an example of a decorative art used for religious and ceremonial purposes by the Ashanti people of Ghana, who belong to the Akan group. Not all the African religious works of art are masks and figures, and the Ashanti people in particular have turned their talent towards the decoration of the cloths, the cups, the bowls and the stools used in the courts of their chiefs and in their rites for the dead.

Plate 37 *Wall of house with mud decoration*. Northern Nigeria.
This form of decoration is typical of the dwelling houses found in Northern Nigeria, particularly in Islamic areas.

Plate 38 *Granary near Kafancan*. Northern Nigeria.
The traditional architecture of Africa (see figure 8) is a subject in itself. In particular the granary huts for storing grain, like huge pots, achieve a beauty and roundness of form which create a lasting impression on the traveller crossing the Western Sudan.

Plate 39 *Ancestral Screen with boat on top*. Kalabari Ijo, Nigeria. Wood. 44½ × 28 in. (102 × 71 cm.). British Museum. London.
Some of the Kalabari Ijo masquerades have been described in the introduction. This is an interesting example of how imported forms such as boats, motor-cars, aeroplanes, are incorporated in masks made for traditional festivals by many of the sculptors throughout Africa, particularly those nearest the coast who have been most exposed to outside influences. Benin sculpture of the sixteenth century, for example, often shows soldiers in Portuguese armour.

Plate 40 *Woman with three children*. Afo, Northern Nigeria. Wood. Height 27 in. (68 cm.). Horniman Museum, London.
This is the most superb example of a fertility figure in the whole of African art. Originally it was attributed to the Yoruba in Nigeria by Major Buxton who collected it on a military expedition in 1906, but then Bernard Fagg pointed out that similar figures existed in a small tribe known as the Afo who live in the hills just north of the River Benue in Northern Nigeria. Very little is known about the Afo who make these carvings. Their villages are remote and inaccessible, and the people will not come anywhere near the roads and the neighbouring towns. During the nineteenth century they lived in large towns, but they were conquered and overrun by the Islamic Fulani. It is possible that much of their art perished at the same time. Only one fertility figure like this one has been seen in the possession of the Afo themselves; but others may be hidden away and only brought out for ceremonies which take place in the hills far away from European and Muslim eyes. Examples in a similar style have been seen or collected in the towns and villages of the neighbouring peoples as much as a hundred miles away, and these peoples say that the Afo made the carvings and that only the Afo possess this skill. It seems probable that the figure is used by the women's secret society at a festival when the first shoots of corn begin to appear above ground. The figures are wrapped in cloths with only the head left visible. Then they are carried on the heads of the bearers to the chief of the women where they are set down in a row outside her compound. The women come and make sacrifices to the figures so that the earth-goddess will help them with the birth of children.

Plate 41 *Wall Decoration*. Johannesburg, South Africa.
This wall was part of a house in Western Native Township, Johannesburg, one of two thousand pulled down in a clearance scheme. Some of them were built in 1920, but with no amenities. Nevertheless people liked living there. One resident said to Professor Julian Beinart of Cape Town: 'Western Native Township was a place of understanding, cohesion. That is why we used to call it Thulwndisville, which literally means "Okay, I heard you".' So the people changed their houses in such a way that the fronts facing the streets would have on them a symbol which would communicate with others. Professor Beinart says that this desire to show their solidarity and cooperation in a community caused the people living there to use a few basic shapes to express a number of simple concepts. A circle could become a watch or a cogwheel to represent an African political party, or it could have radiating lines to represent the sun. A rectangle could become a razor blade, diamonds become butterflies or trees.

Plate 42 *Door from Mozambique*. East Africa.
Professor Beinart has collected photographs of examples of popular art from all over Africa and has found that Mozambique is particularly rich in this art form.

Plate 43 *Painting on Glass*. Nigeria. 24 × 30 in. 61 × 76 cm.). Collection Professor Julian Beinart, Cape Town.
This is a good example of the popular art of the new urban areas in Africa. Sign-writing is a new profession which has emerged to meet local needs for advertising, such as barbers' signs, cinema posters and for decorating lorries. The lion is a favourite emblem, usually appearing as a charming and rather harmless-looking animal. Sign-writers seldom have

any formal art training so their work retains a refreshing and imaginative naivety although the influence of Western advertising is sometimes apparent.

Plate 44 *Painting*. Malangatana Valente. Mozambique, East Africa. Oil on canvas. 36 × 18 in. (91 × 45 cm.). Collection of Professor Gellner, London.
Malangatana Valente has had no formal art instruction, and has never left Mozambique.

Plate 45 *Painting*. Skunder Boghossian. Ethiopia. 18 × 12 in. (45 × 30 cm.). Collection of Dr G. Liersch, Munich.
Skunder now lives in Addis Ababa, but has studied in London and lived for a long time in Paris. He has had exhibitions in Paris, Munich and New York.

Plate 46 *The Woman, the Bird and the Pomegranate*. Ibrahim Salahi. Sudan. Oil on canvas. 30 × 24 in. (76 × 61 cm.). Artist's Collection.
Ibrahim Salahi is an example of a modern African painter who has been to art schools, such as the Slade School in London, and has worked and exhibited in Paris, Munich and New York.

Plate 47 *Man Hanging from a Tree*. Jimo Akolo. Nigeria. Oil on canvas. 48 × 60 in. (121 × 182 cm.). Artist's Collection.
Another modern African painter who has worked and exhibited in London and studied in the University of Indiana in the United States.

Plate 48 *King Cock in Ibembe Forest*. Twins Seven Seven. Nigeria. Oil on canvas. 30 × 36 in. (76 × 91 cm.). Artist's Collection.
Twins Seven Seven, whose real name is Taiwo Olaniyi, was introduced to painting by Ulli Beier, who met him when he was employed as a dancer by a native herbalist. His dancing is grotesque and bizarre, a cross between dance and mime. In 1964 he joined Georgina Beier's experimental art school at Oshogbo, where his work stood out from the rest because his approach was so different. Ulli Beier wrote in *Black Orpheus No 22*: 'the stories he told with his pictures were so similar to what we have in Amos Tutuola's books that we asked him to illustrate Tutuola... They both seem to live in the same world of ghosts and spirits... His manner of working is unbelievably direct. He does not think about form or composition. He has a lot to say and puts it straight down'.

Plate 49 *Mother Earth and Children*. Yemi Bisiri. Bronze. Height 15 in. (38 cm.). Artist's Collection.
Yemi Bisiri is a traditional Yoruba sculptor who casts in bronze, mainly for the Ogboni cult. He has been encouraged by Ulli Beier at Oshogbo, and his art shows a new element of surrealism compared with that found in earlier work.

Plate 50 *Friends*. Asiru Olatunde. Aluminium panel. 36 × 24 in. (91 × 61 cm.). Artist's Collection.
Asiru Olatunde is a Yoruba blacksmith, who was making jewellery and small ornaments for tourists when he was discovered at Oshogbo by Ulli Beier. Beier encouraged him to work on a large scale on sheets of copper and aluminium, and this is the result. Now he sells almost all the work he can produce, especially to the United States.

Plate 51 *Nuba Woman with Cicatrisation*. Nuba, Sudan.
Cicatrisation patterns are a feature of body ornament over most of Africa. Similar patterns appear on doors, pots, calabashes, stools and other objects. It is sometimes used as a form of initiation at puberty. The marks are made by cutting the skin and rubbing ash into the cuts to achieve a raised effect.

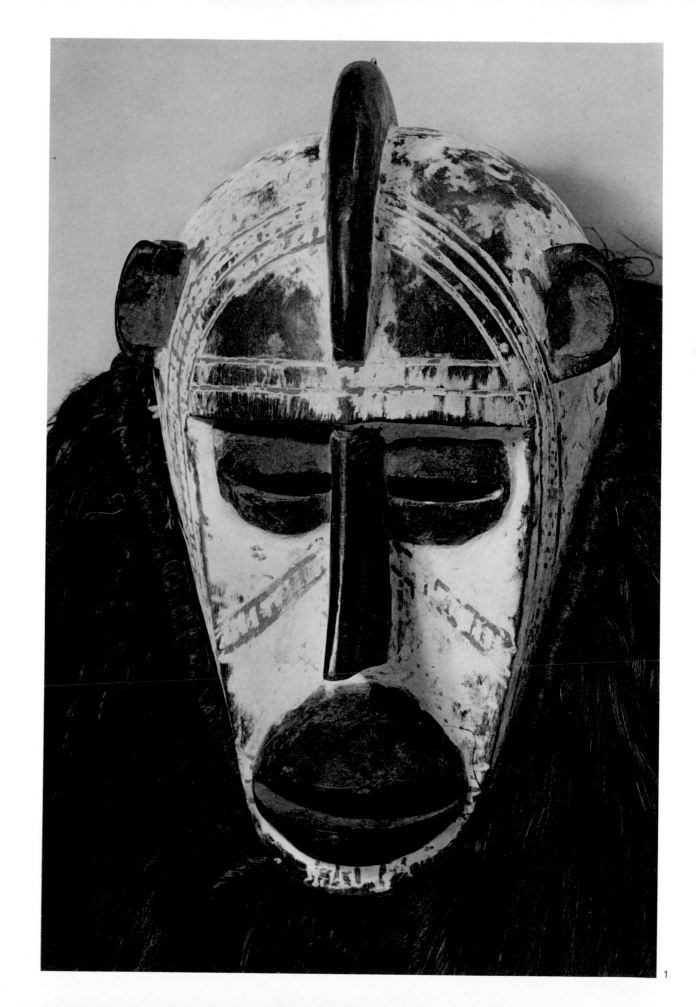

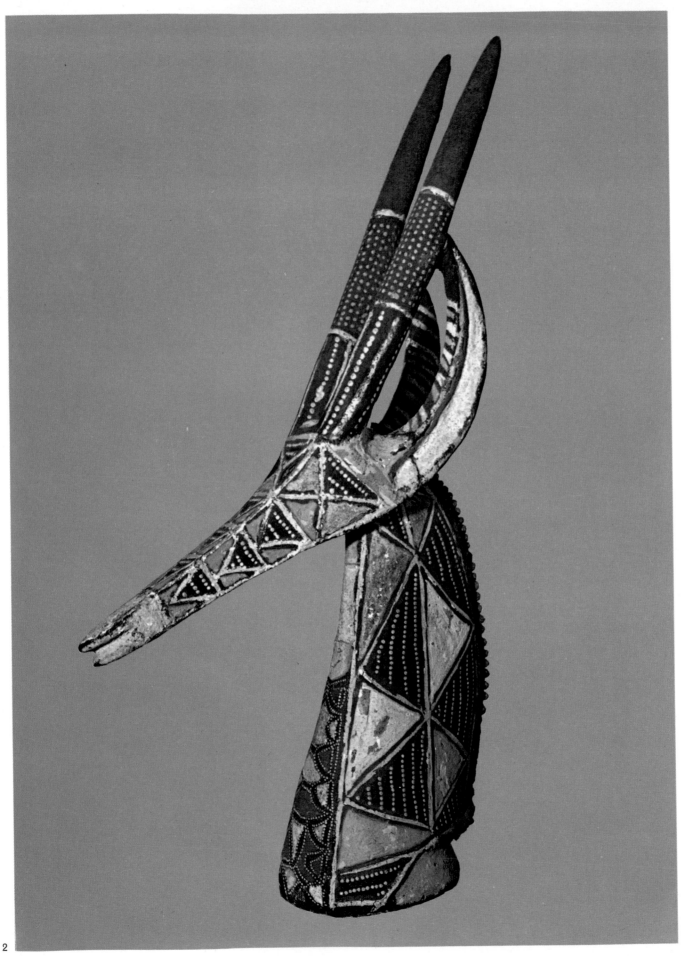

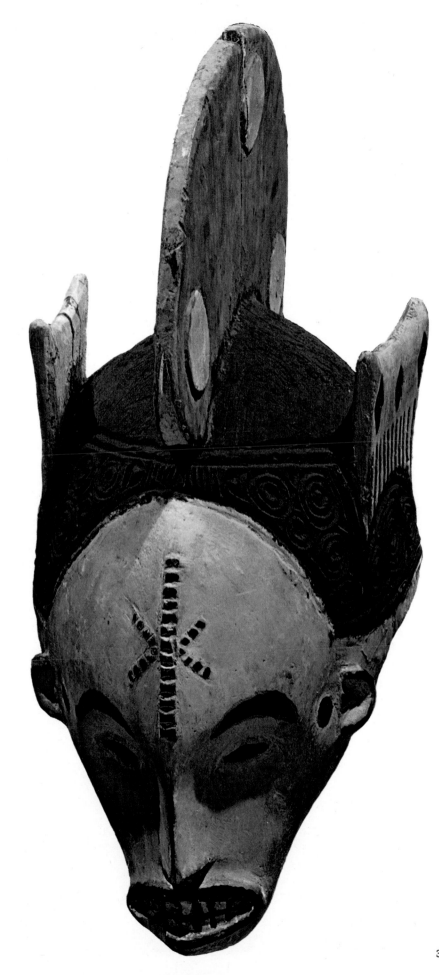

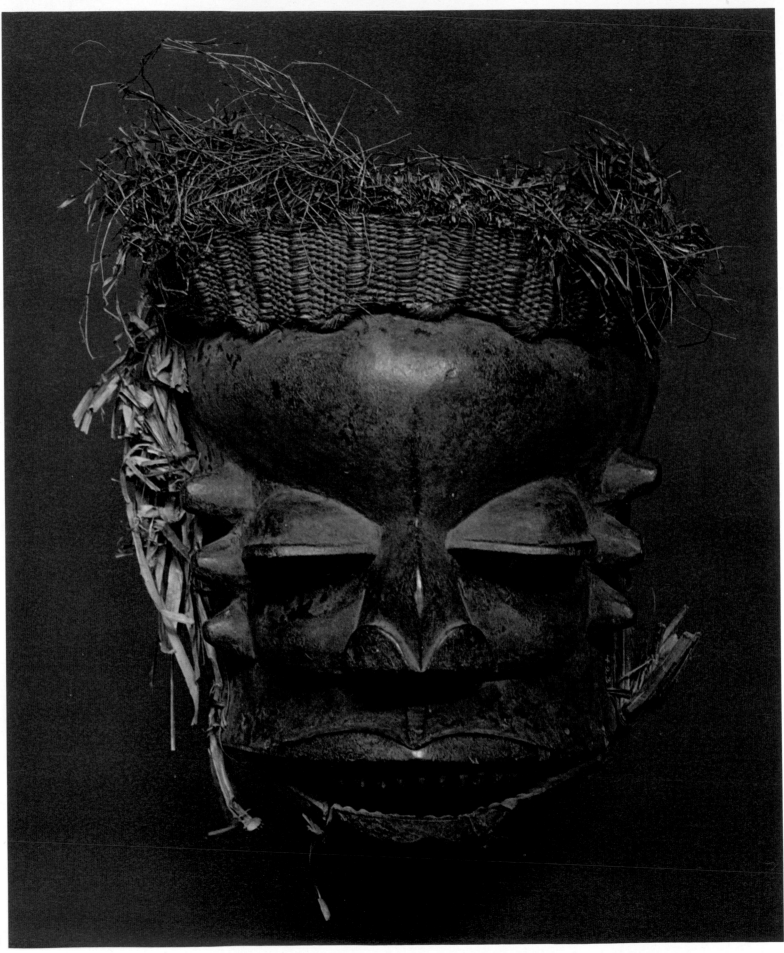

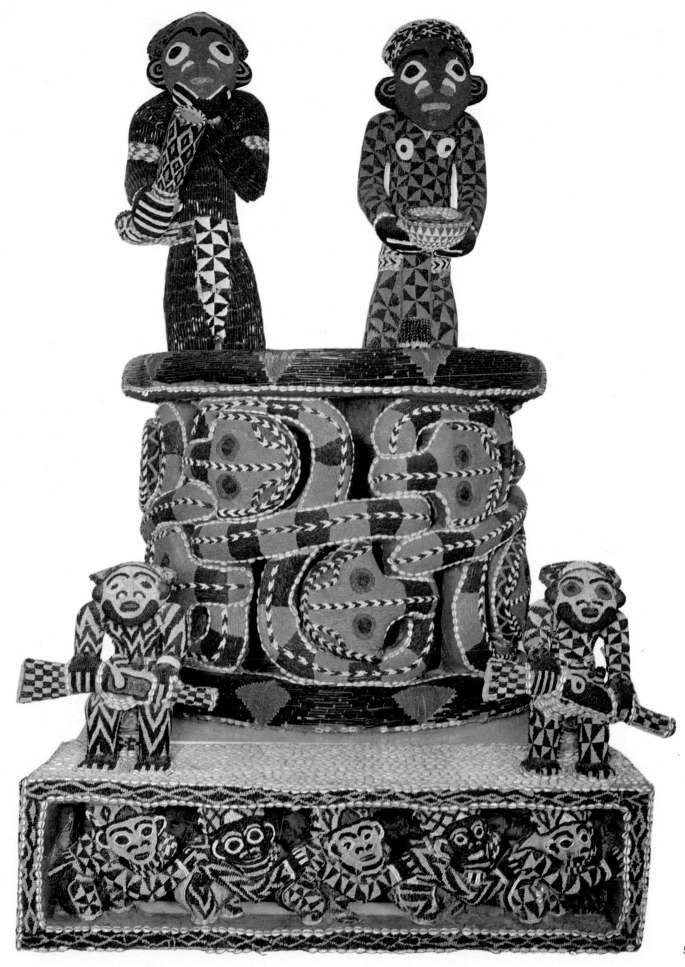

5

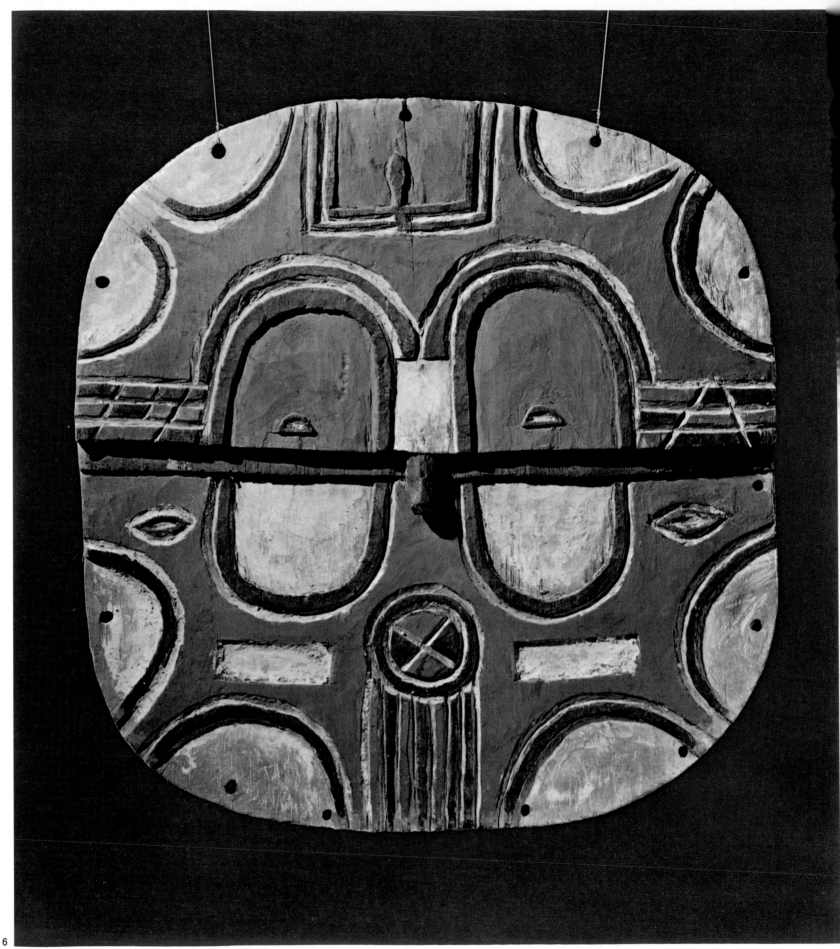

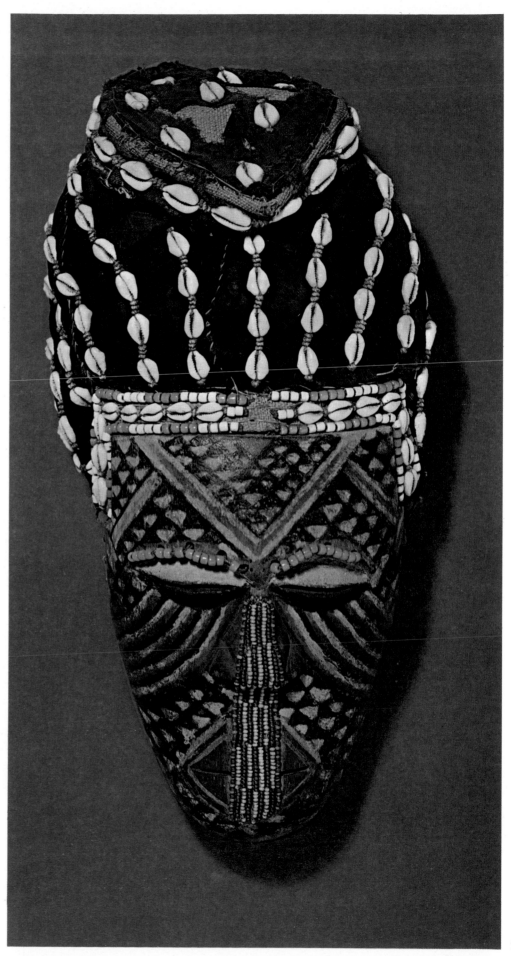

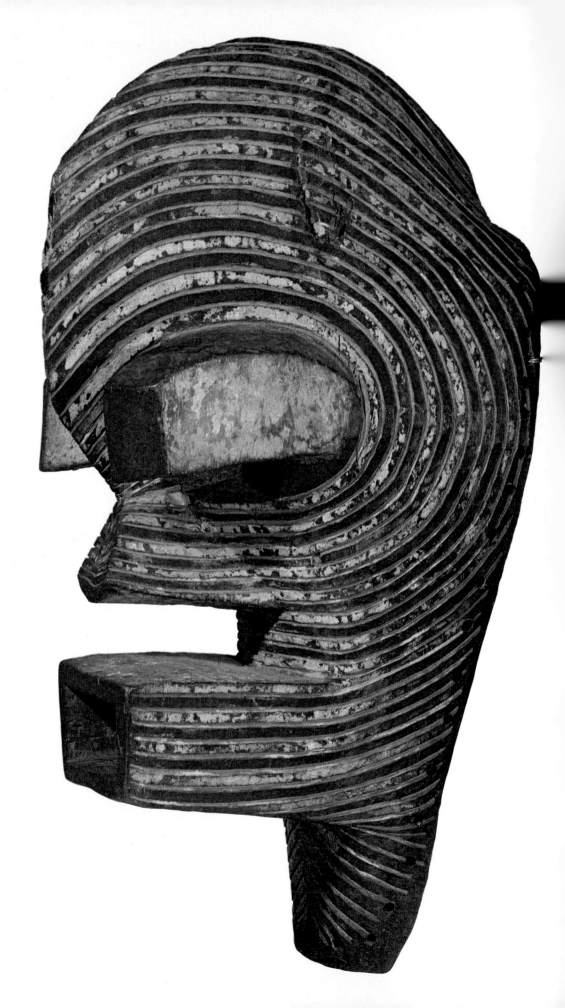

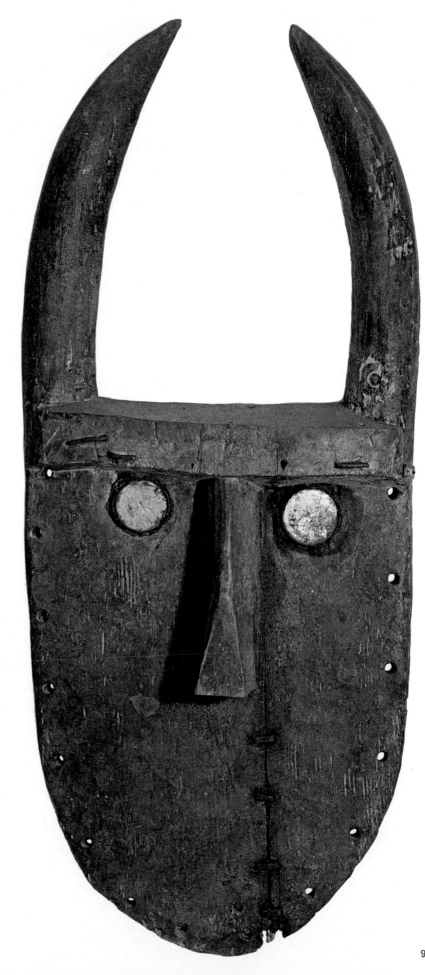

9

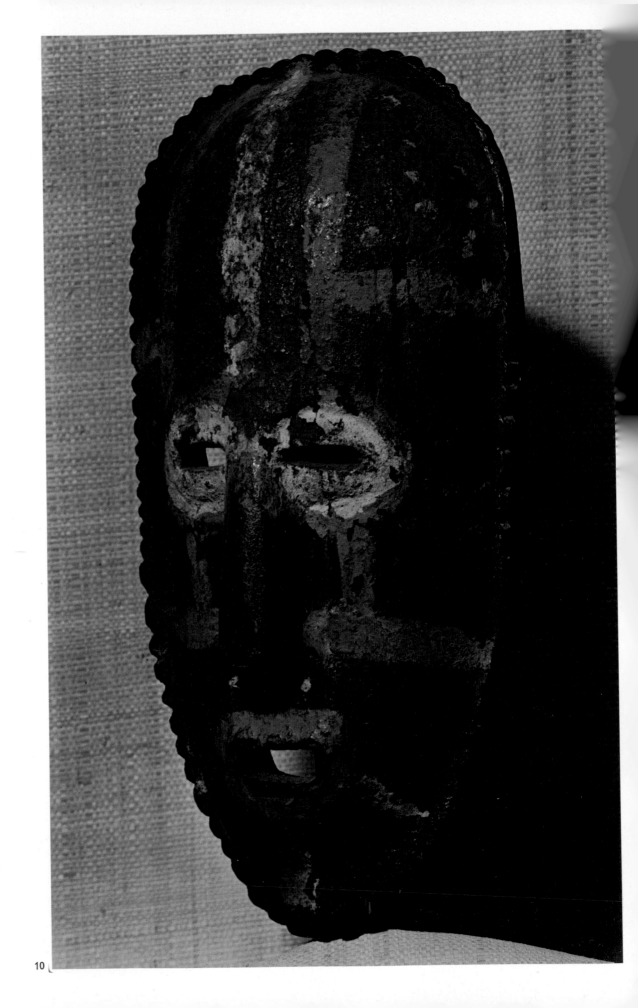

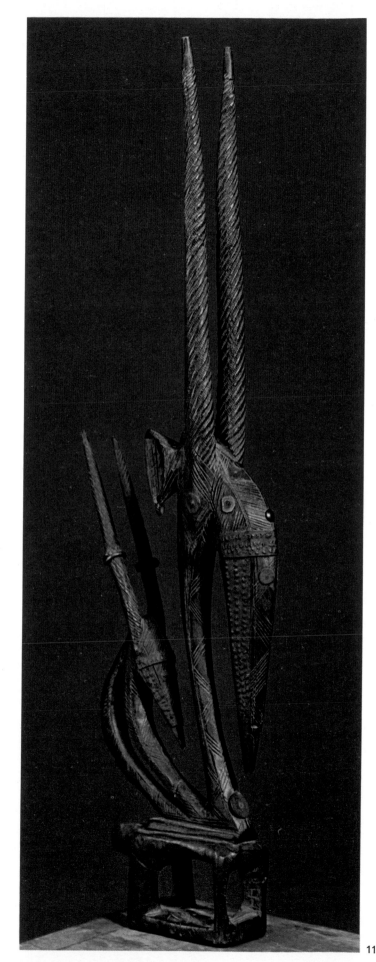

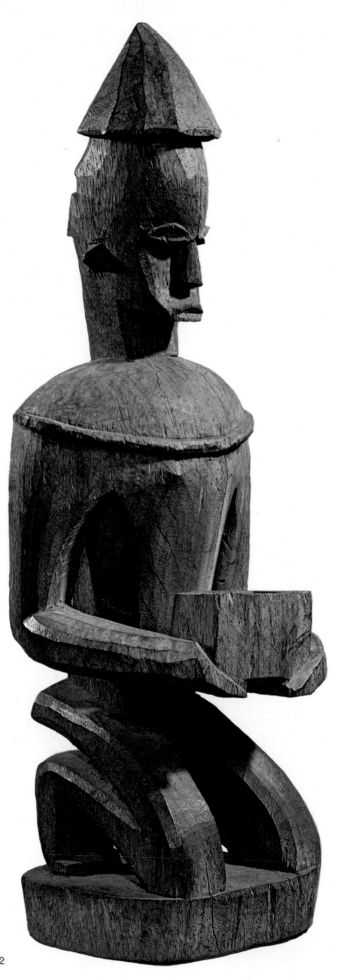

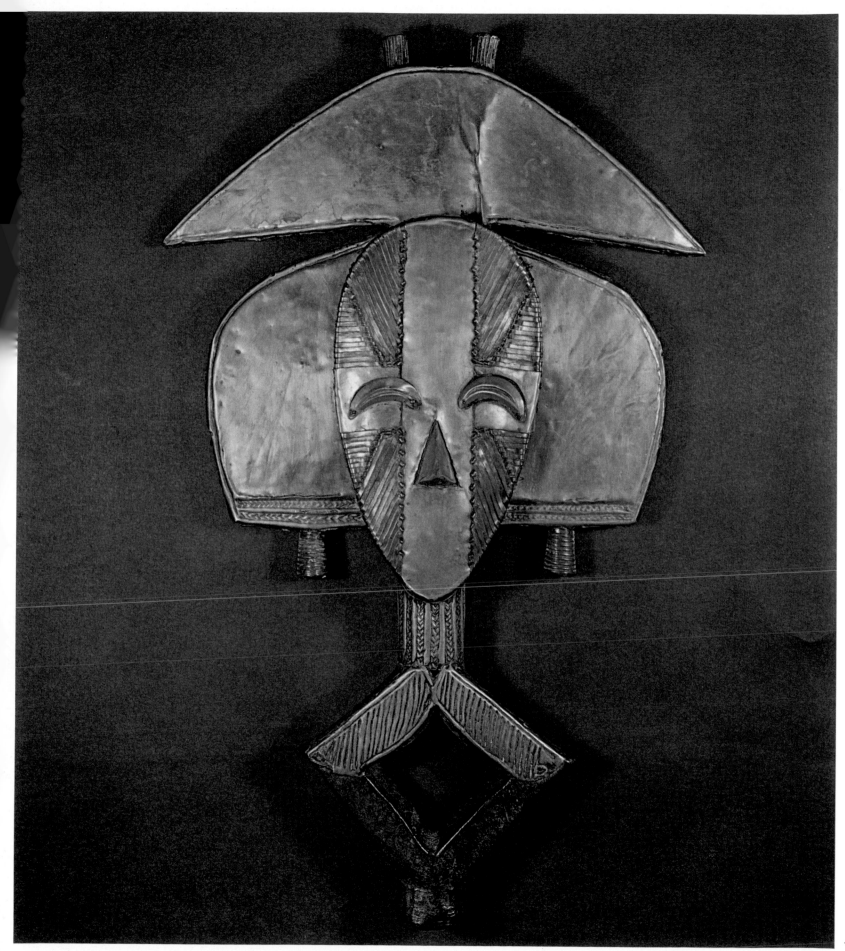

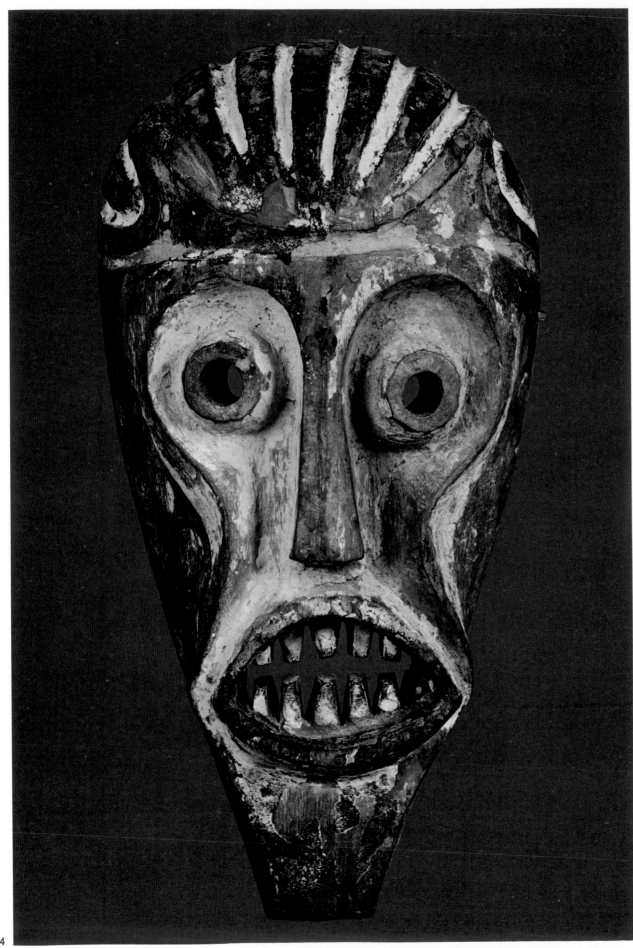

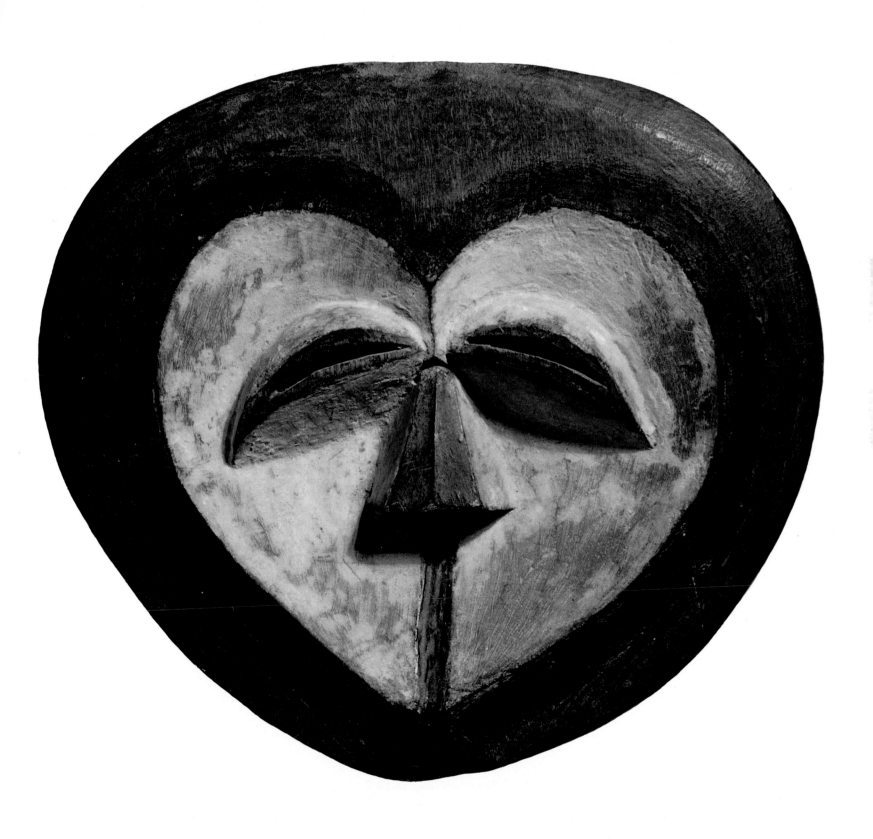

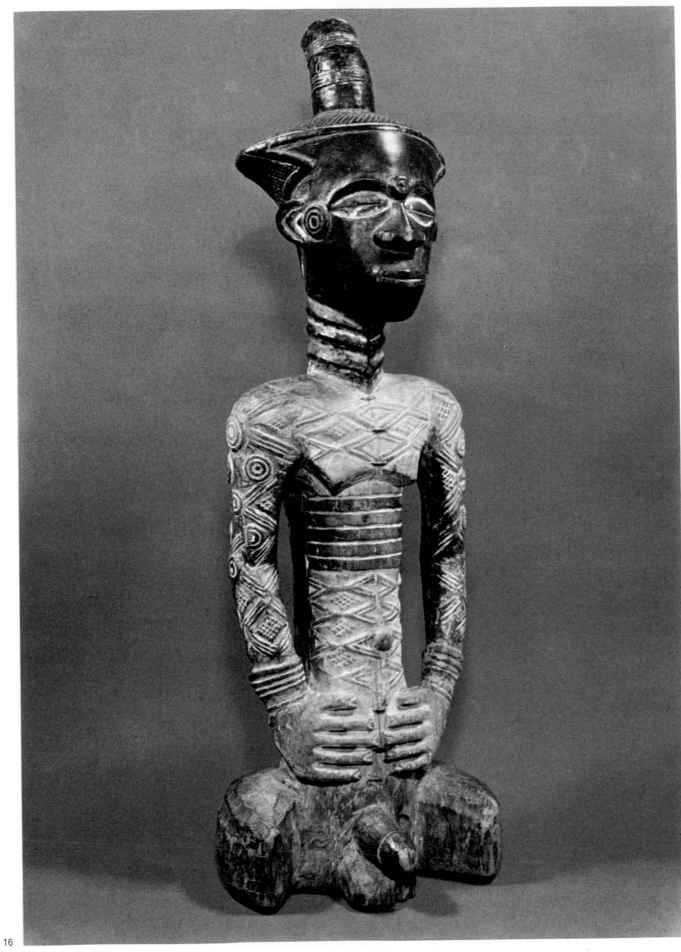

16

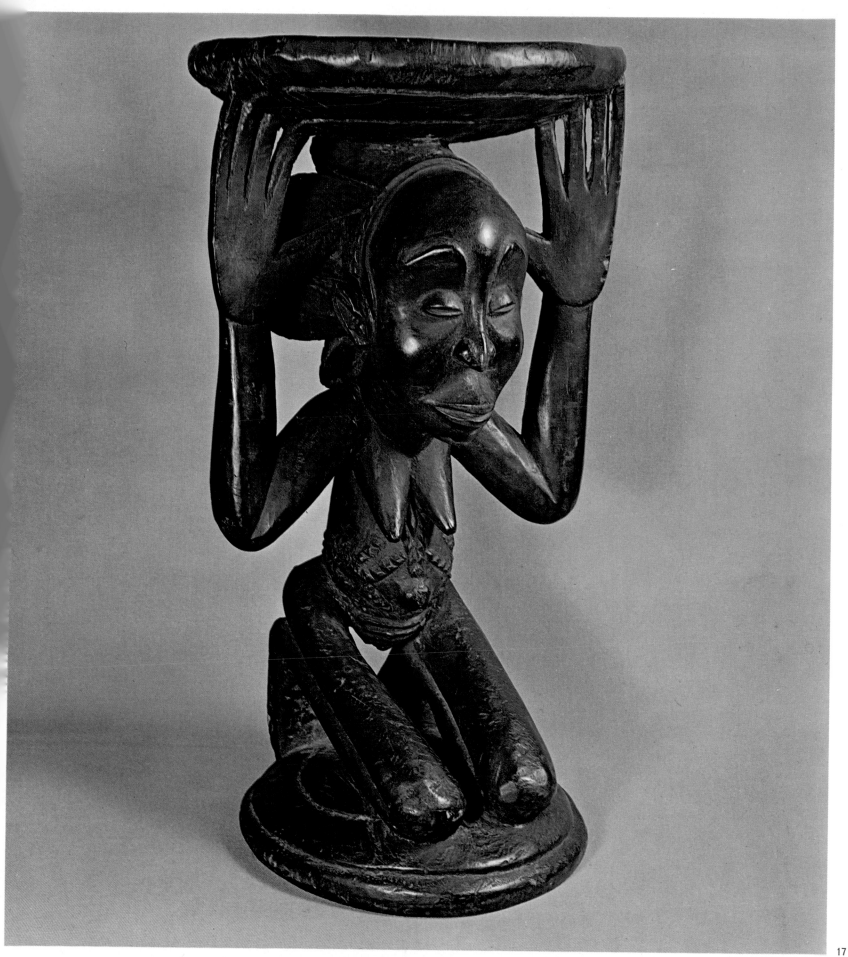

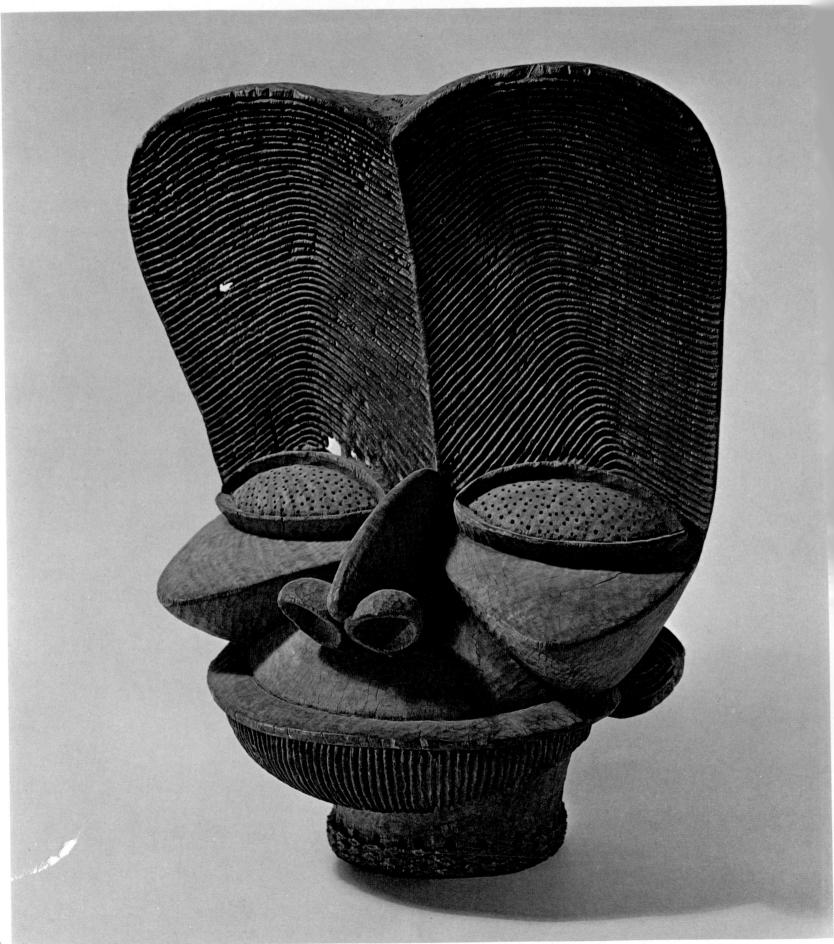

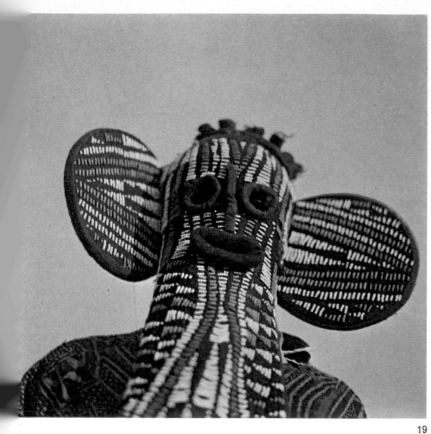

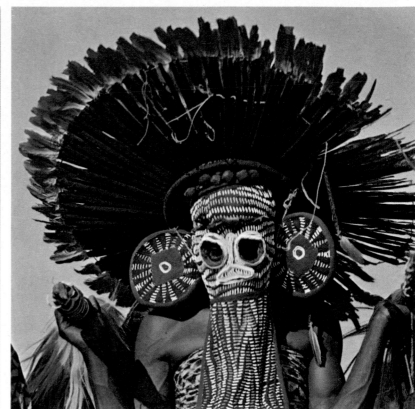

19

20

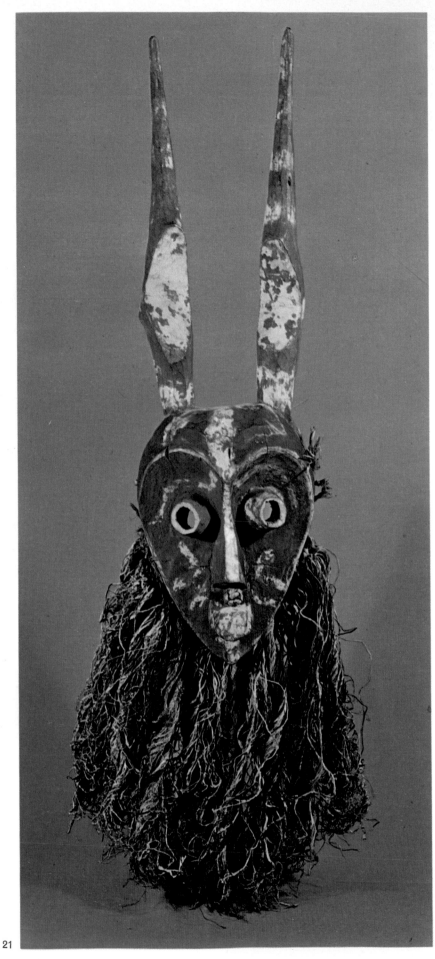

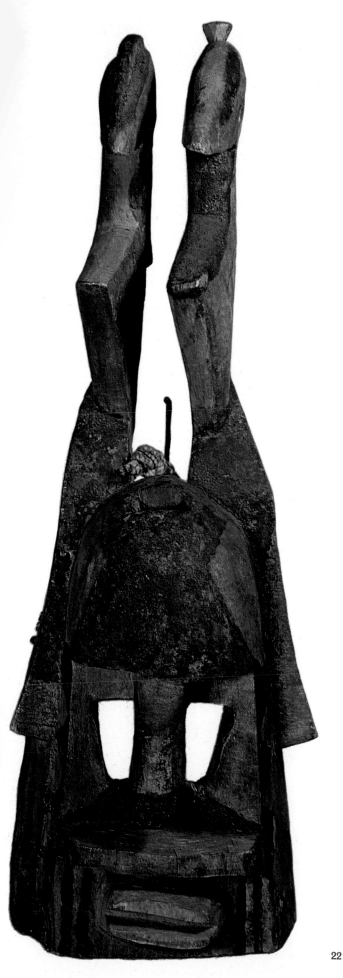

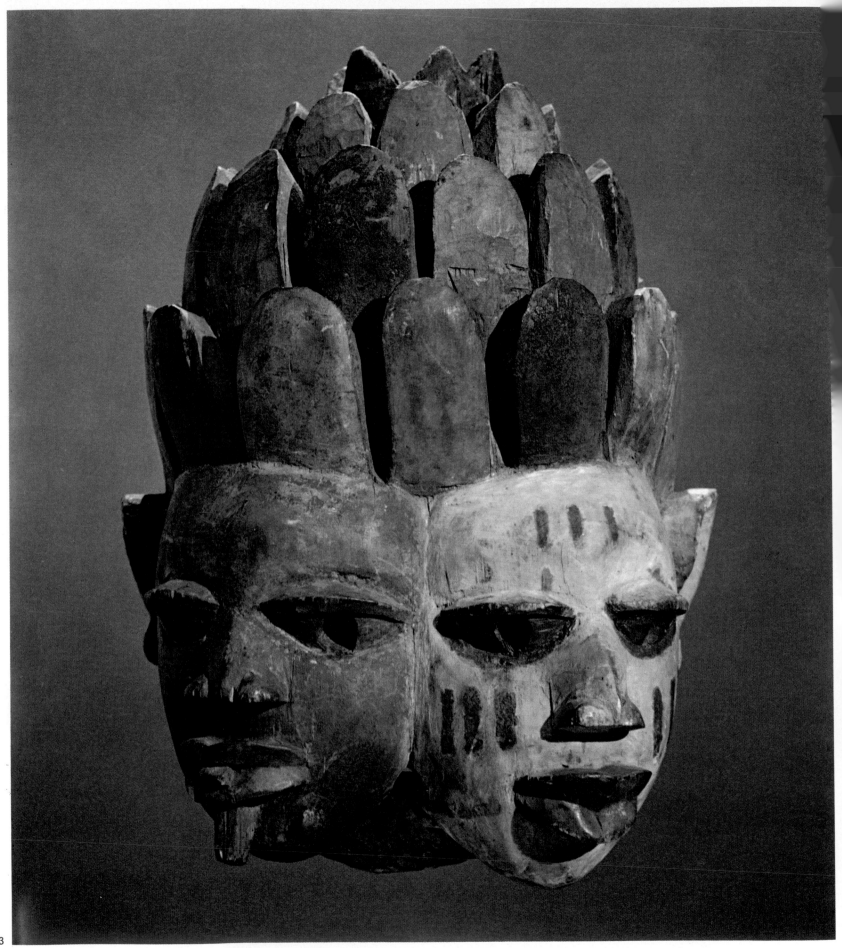

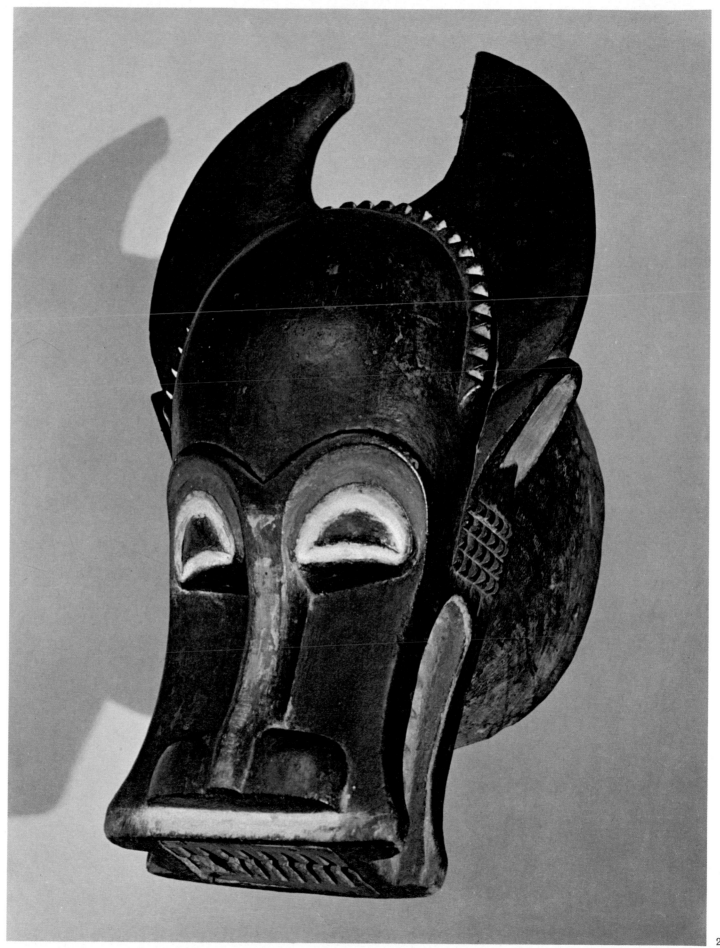

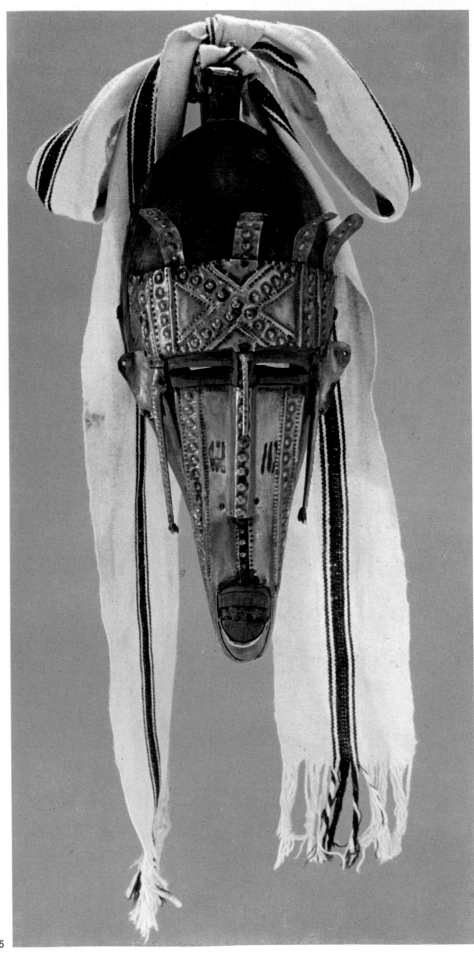

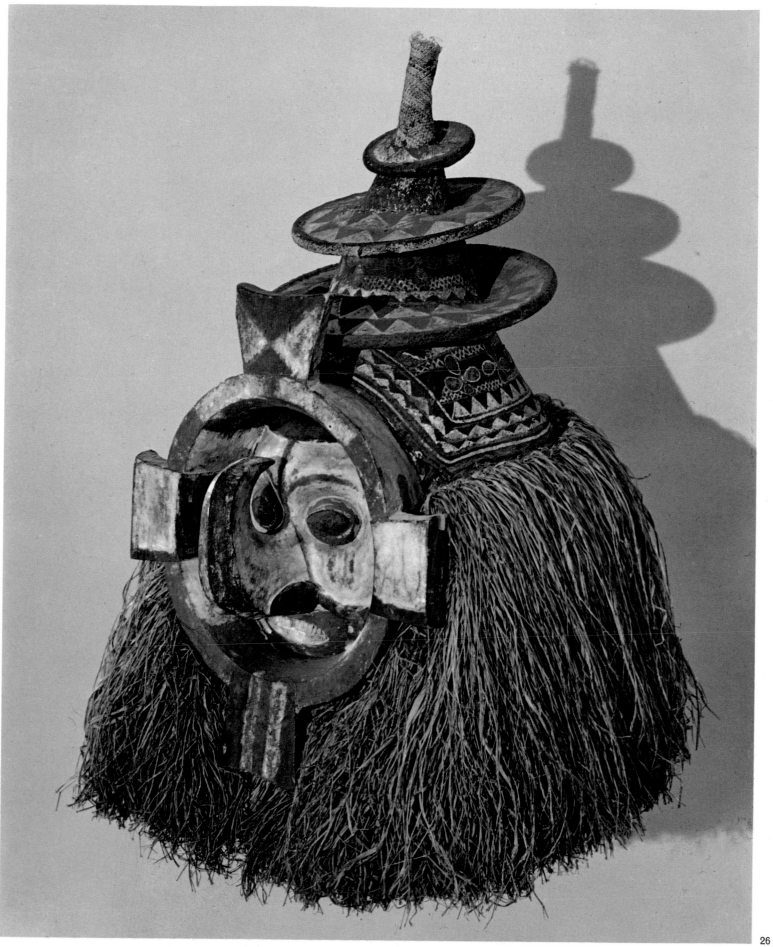

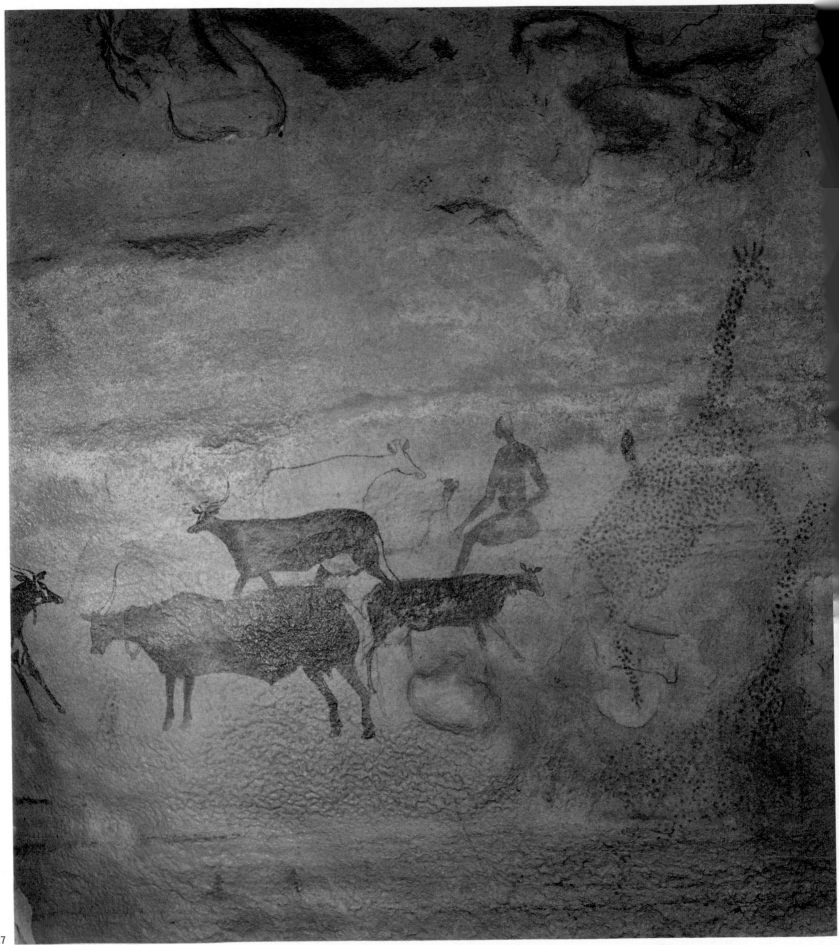

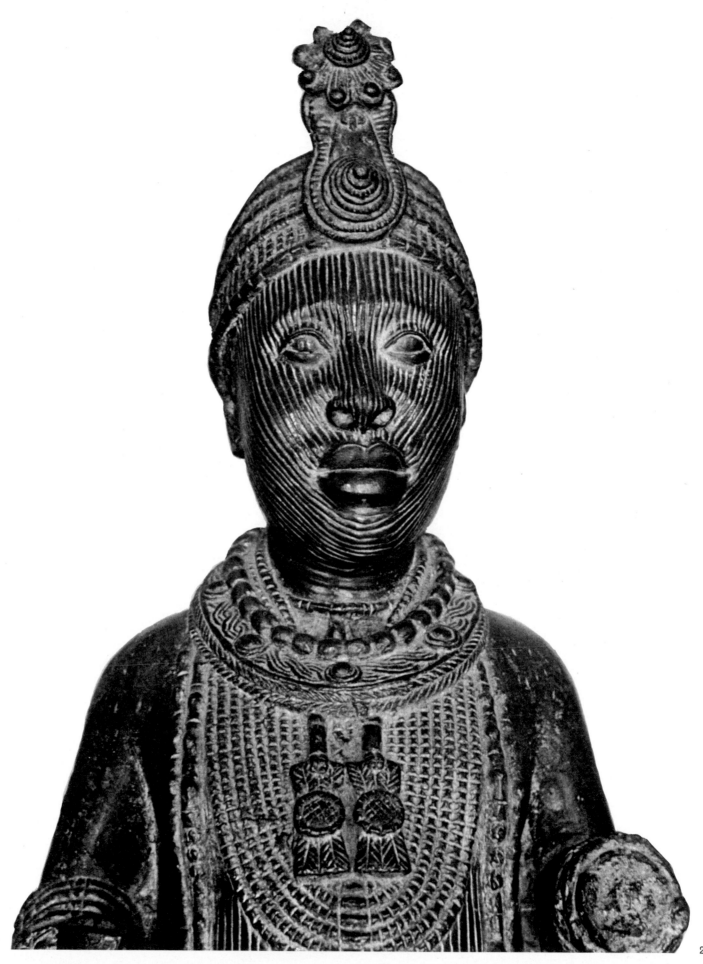

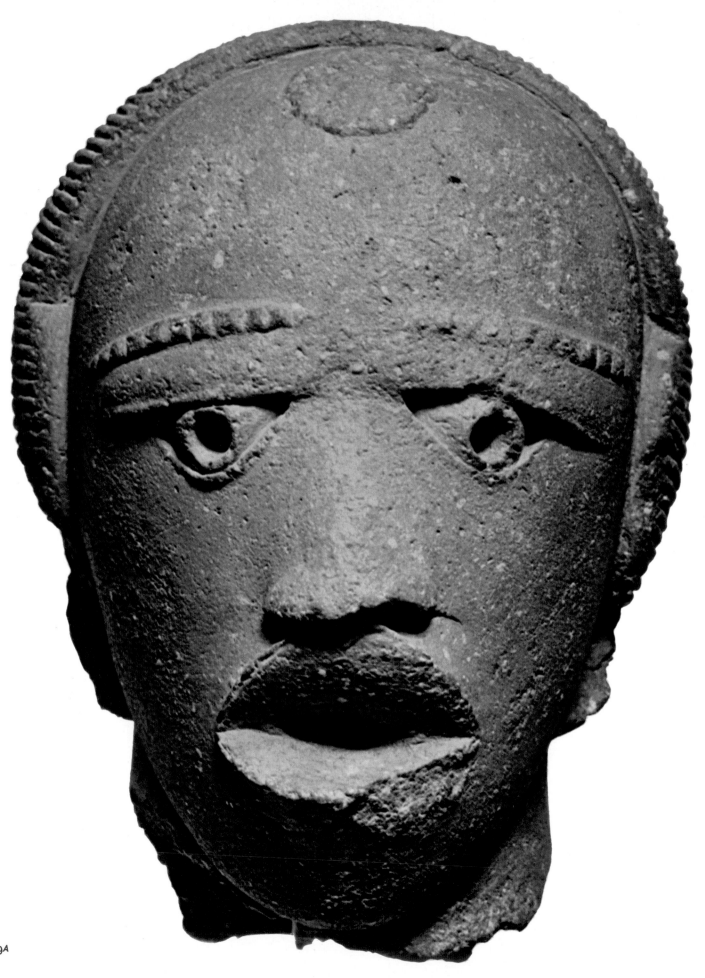

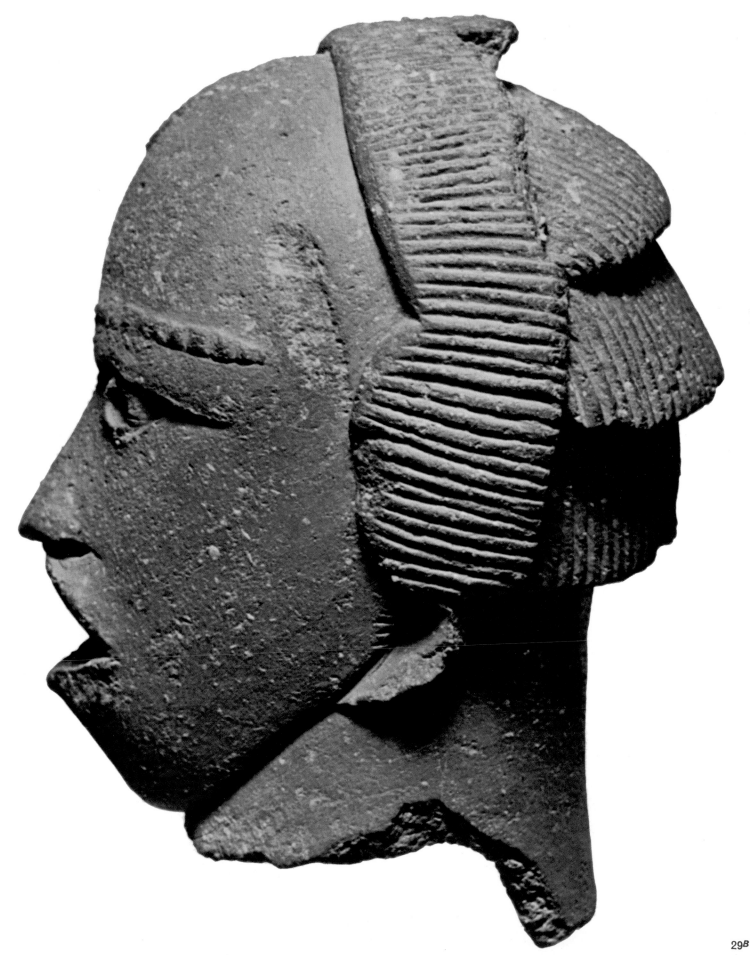

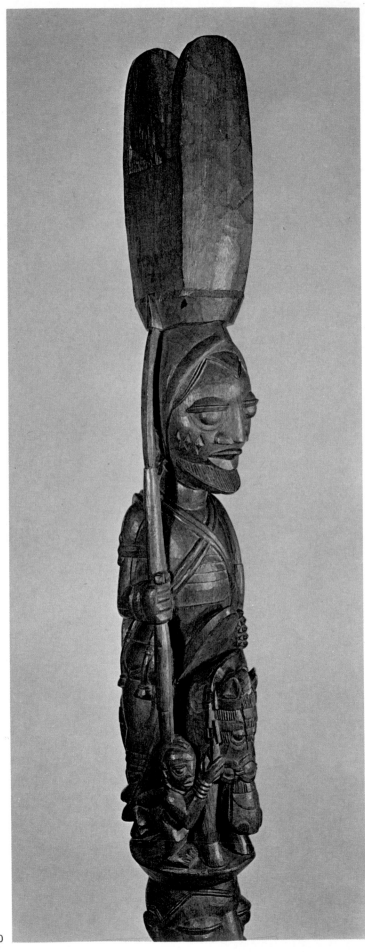

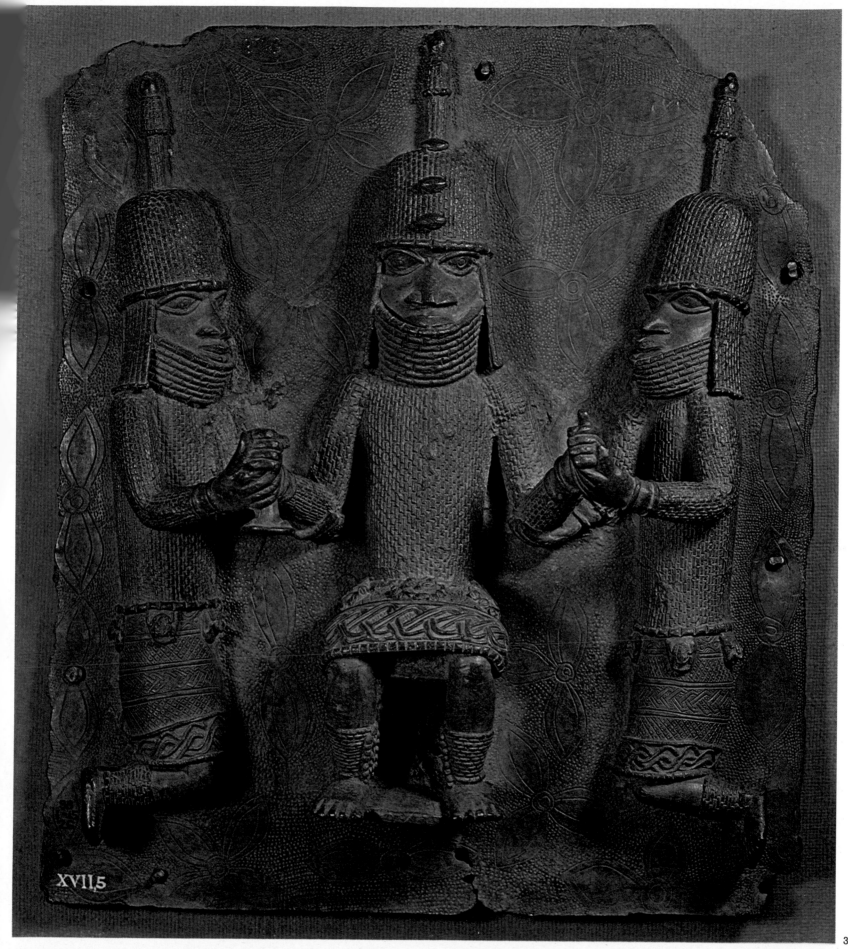

XVII,5

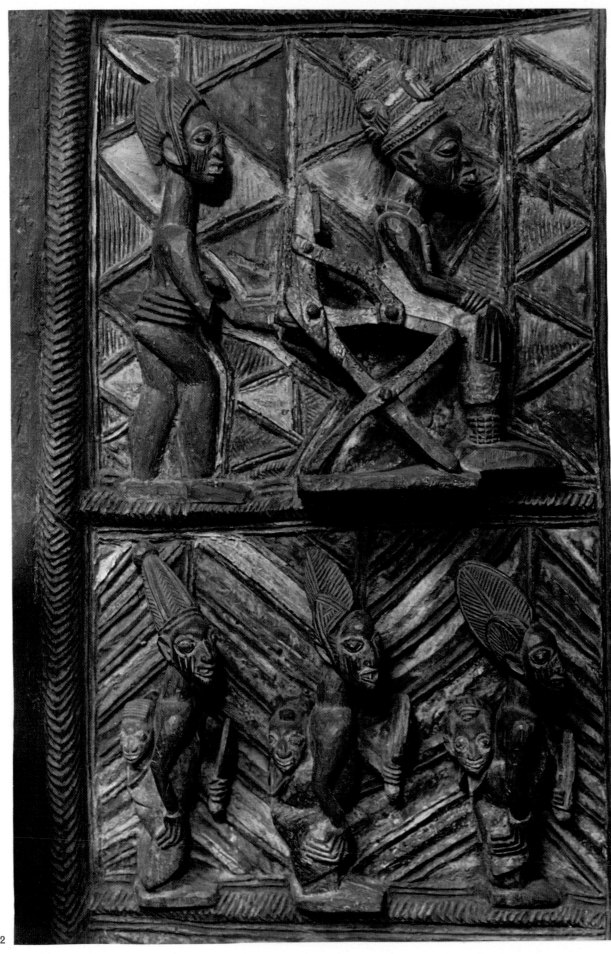

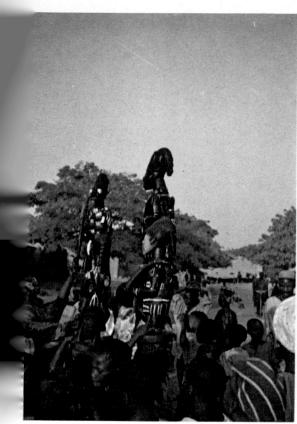

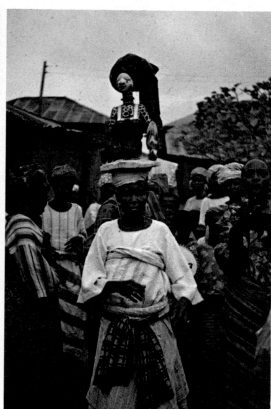

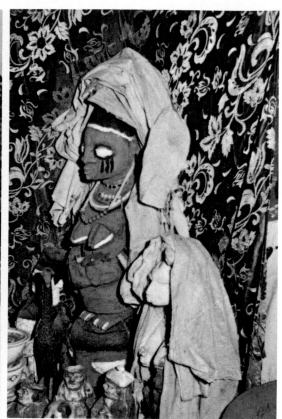

33

34

35

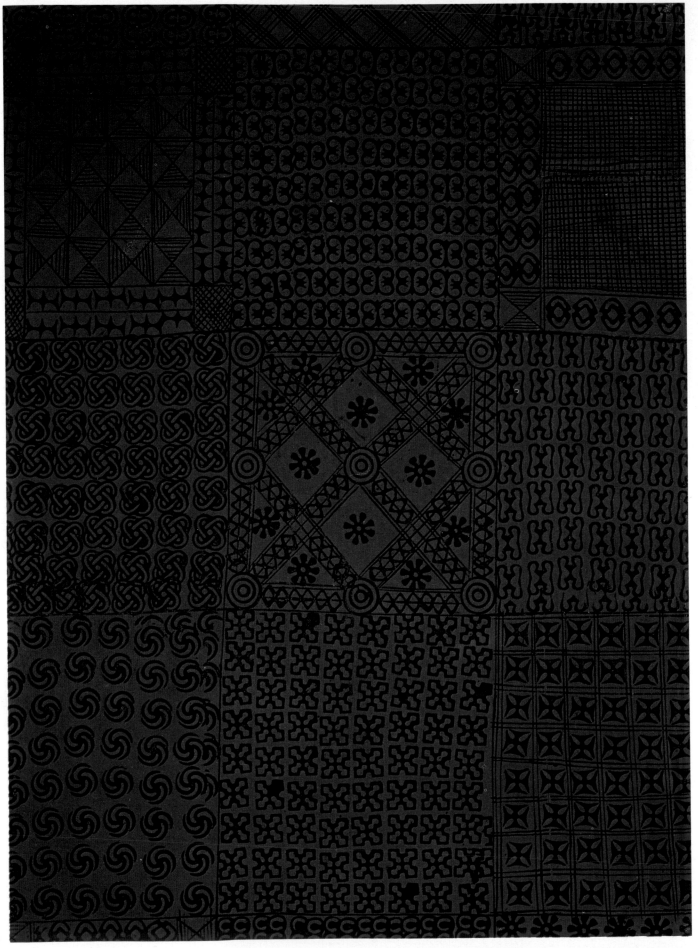

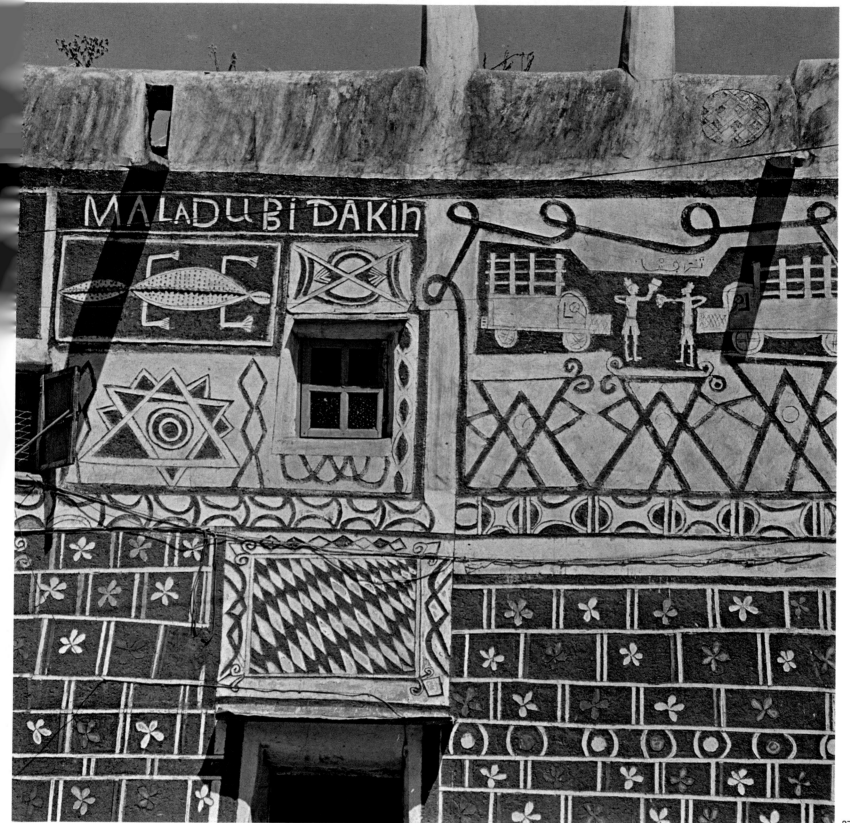

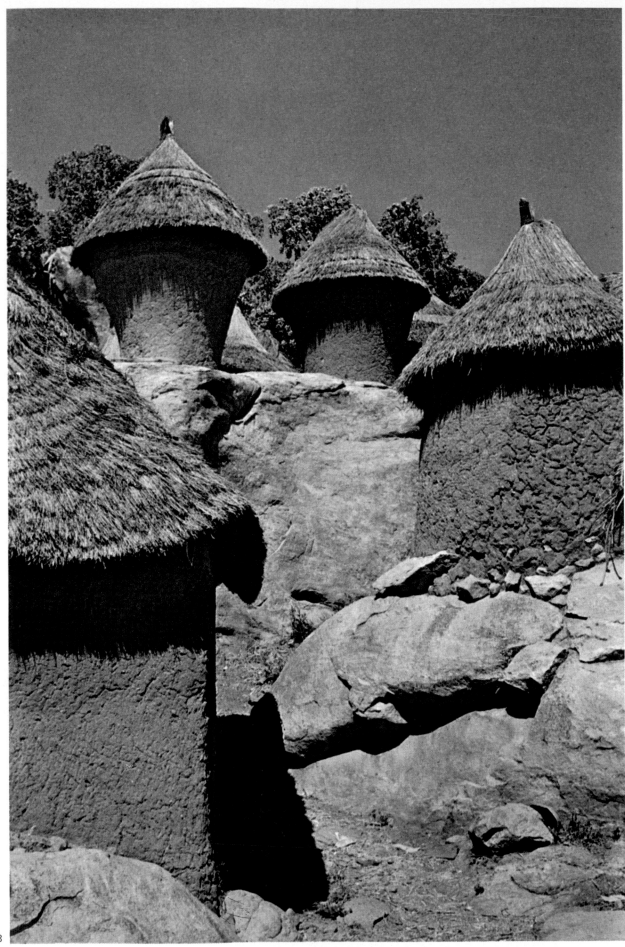

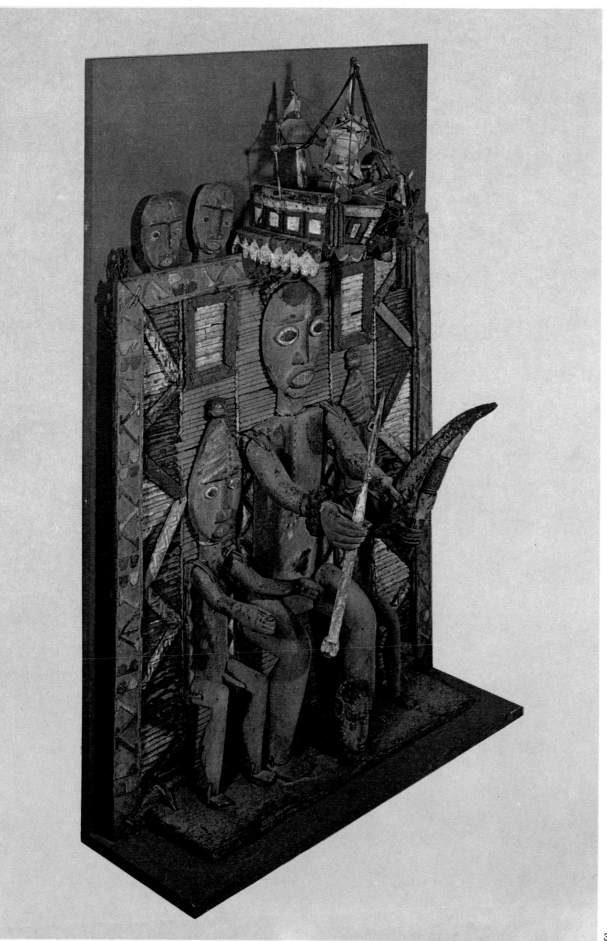

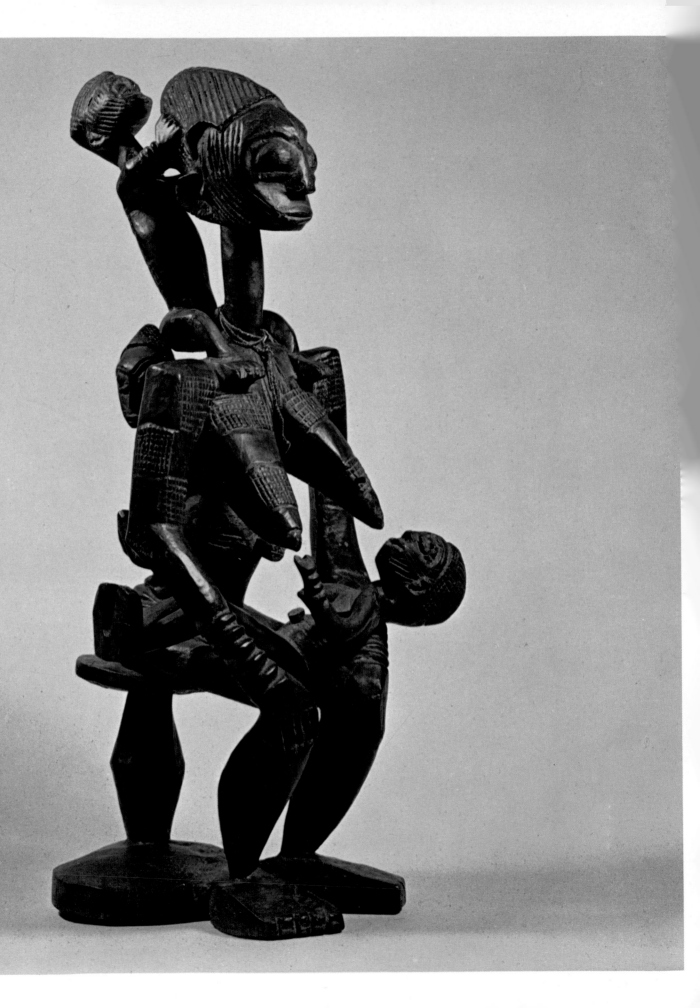

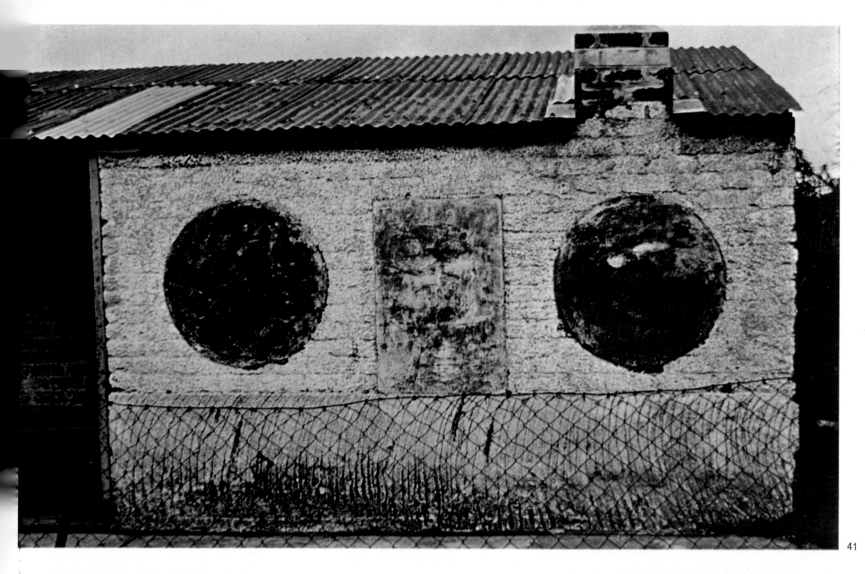

41

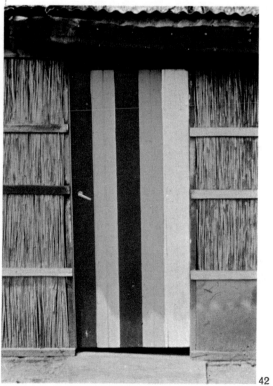

42

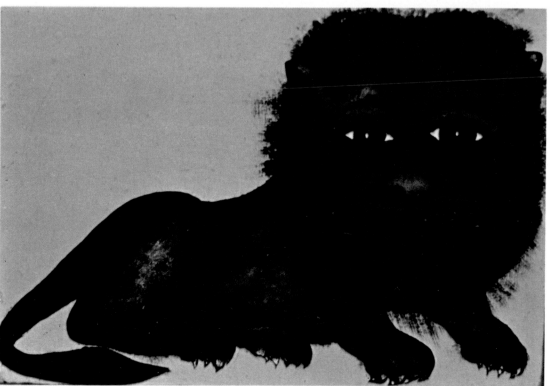

43

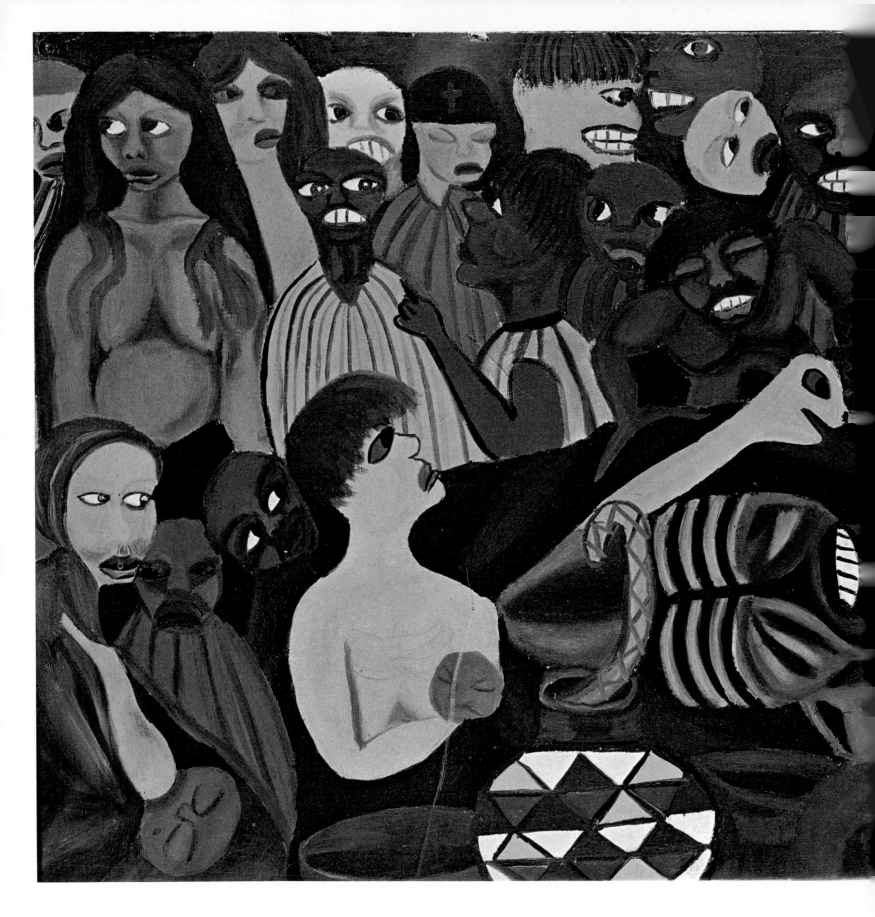

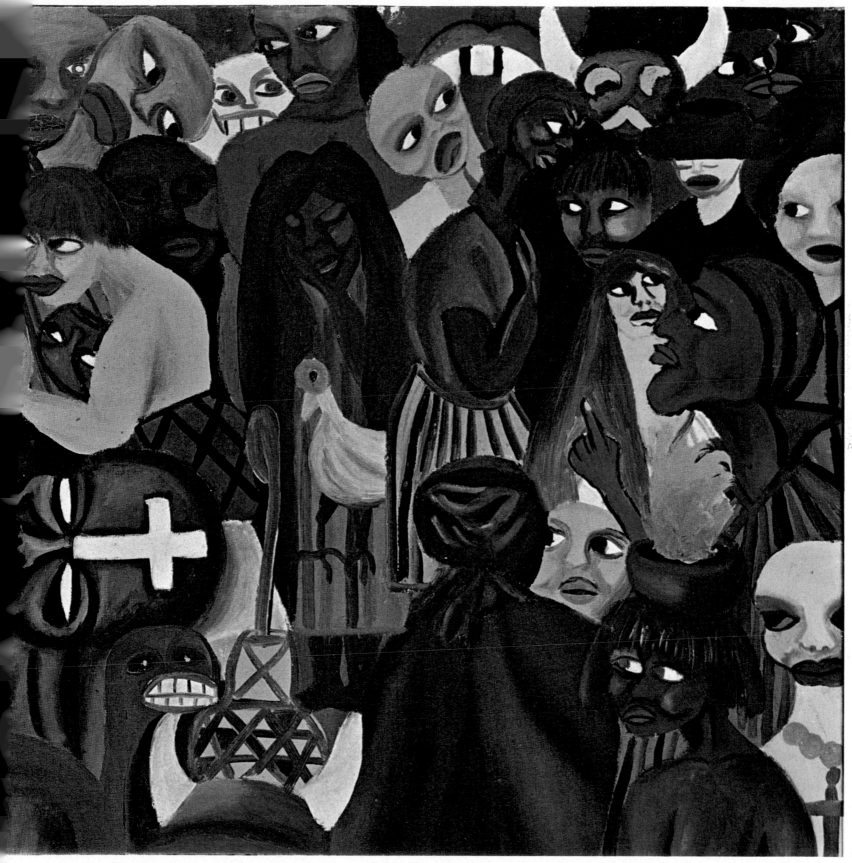

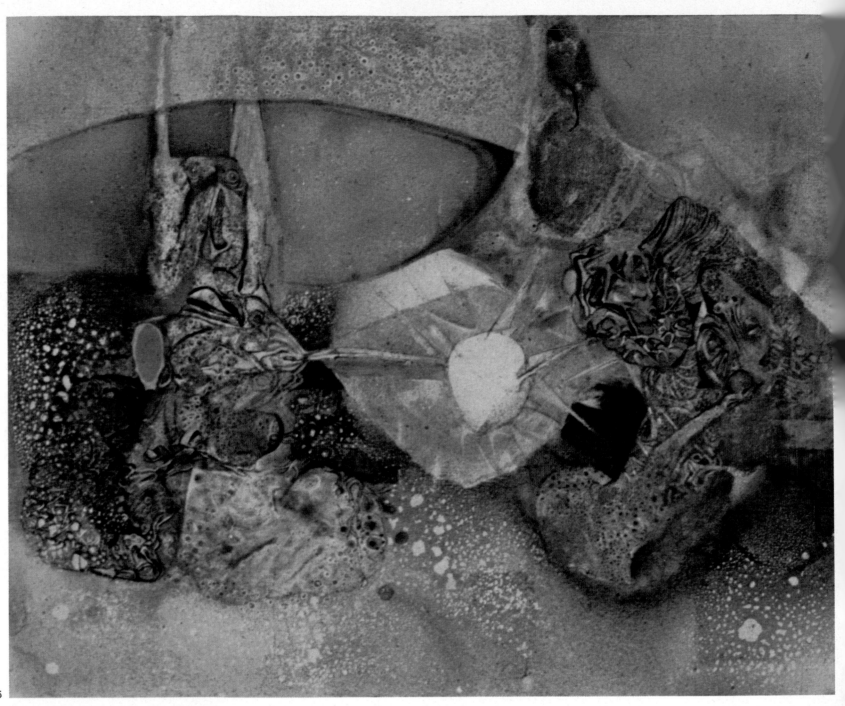

45

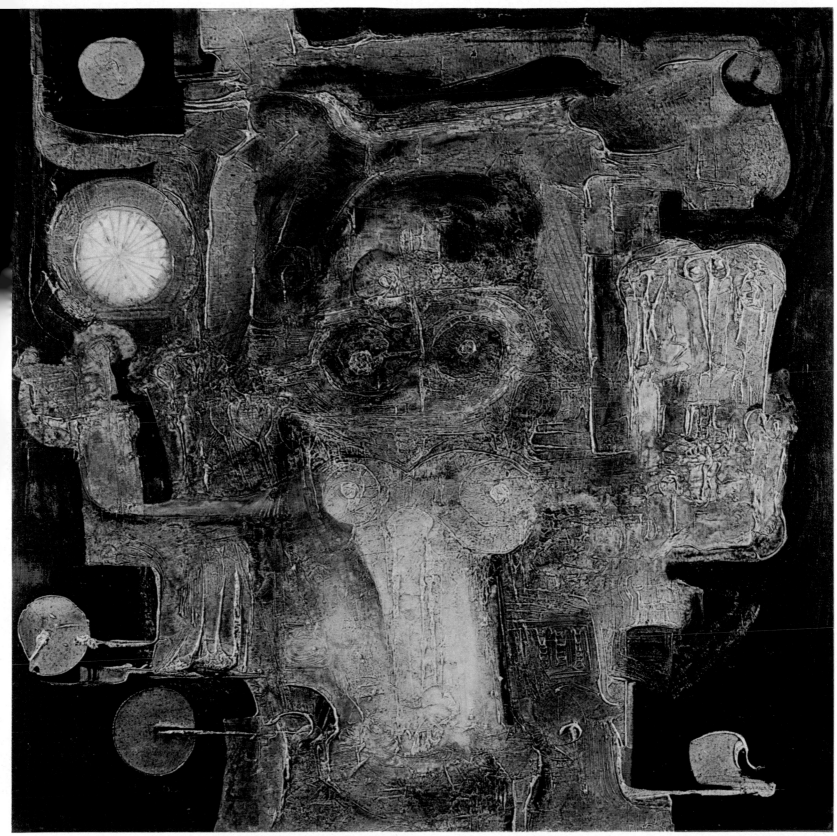

46

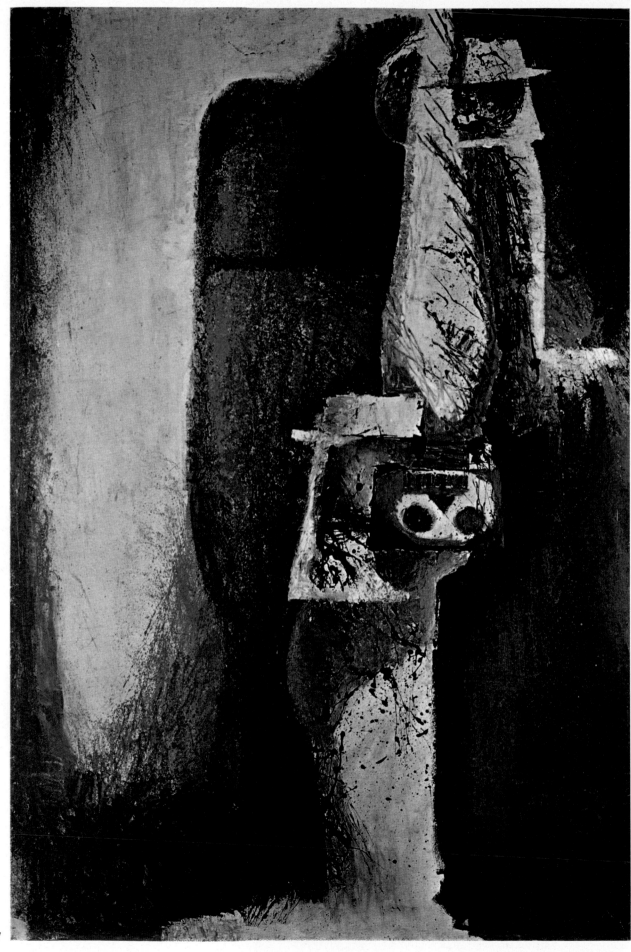

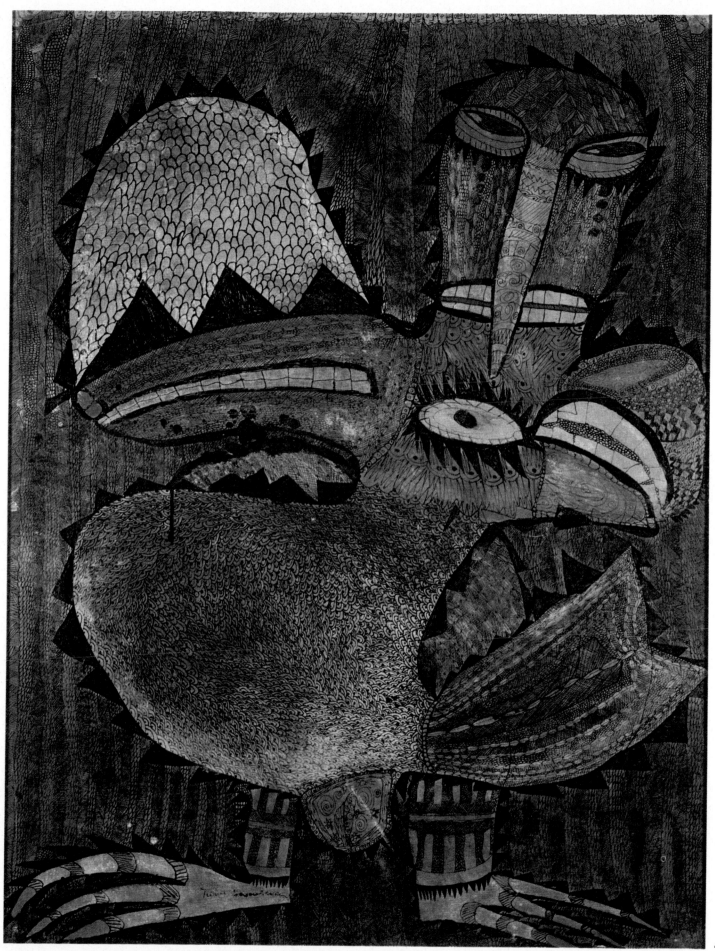

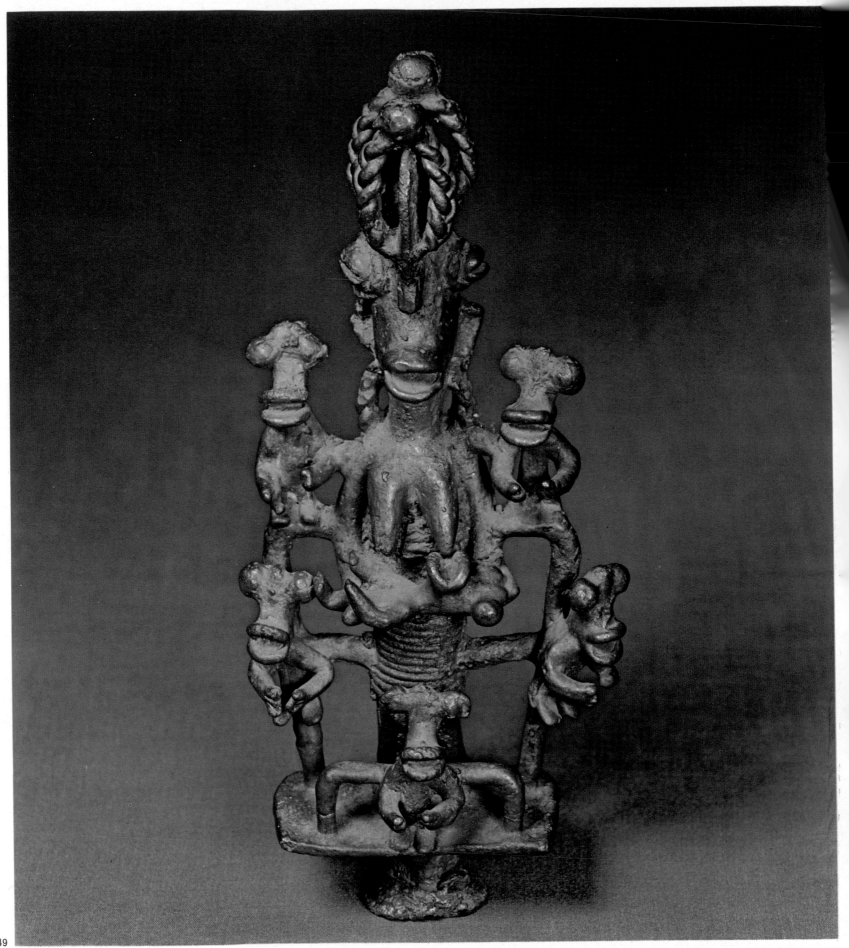

49

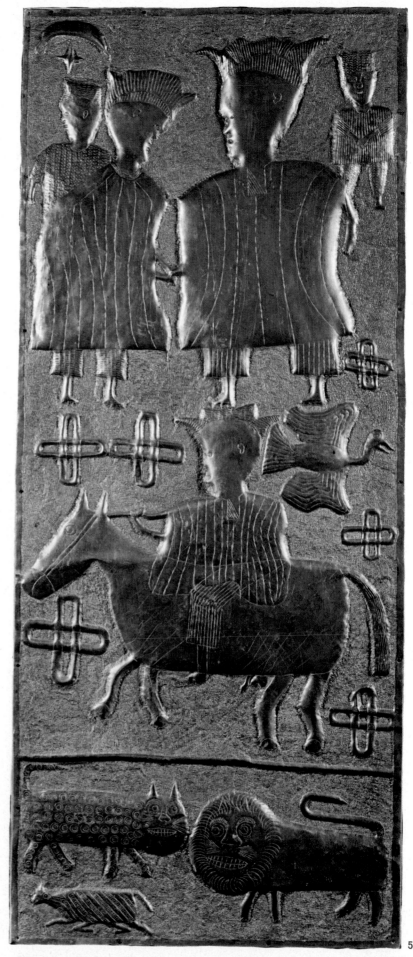

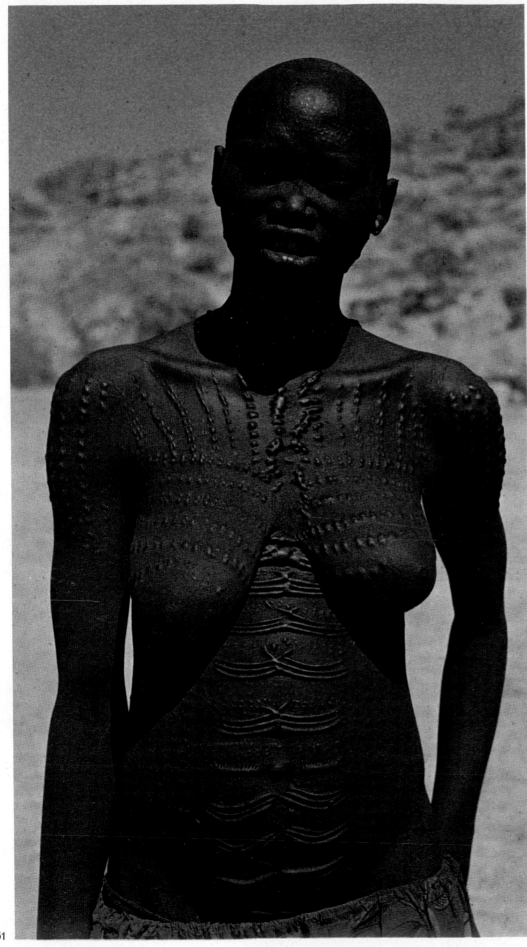